MW01226321

Moving mountains in India, drinking tea in Tbilisi:

A LIFETIME'S SERVICE IN GLOBAL DEVELOPMENT

Moving mountains in India, drinking tea in Tbilisi:
A LIFETIME'S SERVICE IN GLOBAL DEVELOPMENT

YUN-CHONG PAN

BAYEUX

Moving mountains in India, drinking tea in Tbilisi : a lifetime's
service in global development
© 2010 by Bayeux Arts, Inc.
119 Stratton Crescent SW,
Calgary, Canada T3H 1T7
www.bayeux.com

Library and Archives Canada Cataloguing in Publication

Pan, Yun-Chong
         Moving mountains in India, drinking tea in Tbilisi : a lifetime's
service in global development / Yun-Chong Pan.

ISBN 978-1-897411-23-0

        1. Pan, Yun-Chong. 2. Economic assistance, Canadian.
3. Canadians--Foreign countries--Biography. I. Title.

HC79.E44P35 2010   338.91'710092   C2010-904404-5

First Printing: September 2010
Printed in Canada at Marquis Book Printing Inc.
Cover Design: Hadi Farahani
Text Design: Dave Casey

The ongoing publishing activities of Bayeux Arts, under its "Bayeux" and "Gondolier" imprints,
are supported by the Canada Council for the Arts, the Alberta Foundation for the Arts, and the
Government of Canada through the Book Publishing Industry Development Program.

 Canada Council   Conseil des Arts
        for the Arts   du Canada

 Alberta
Foundation
for the Arts

 Canadian Patrimoine
Heritage canadien
Book Publishing Industry Development Program

PREFACE

On the subject of randomness in the universe, Albert Einstein once wrote to a colleague, "God does not play dice with the universe." True in physics, however, God did play dice with my life. I encountered many of the most significant people and events in my life by accident, without any regard to my wishes. My only part in the process was to act, to see things through after these accidents, often with astonishing results.

Of course, I am not the only one to feel the power of accidents in life. Goethe started his autobiography, *Out of My Life: Poetry and Reality* with the alignment of the stars on his birthday. For me, the roll of the dice began with my birthday, which was accidentally changed by pure chance. My grandfather was supposed to return from Japan before the day I was due. But I arrived early, on February 18, 1935. My father waited two days for my grandfather to come home and give me a name. Consequently, my birth certificate states my date of birth as February 20, 1935. Many Asians have two birthdays, one according to the lunar calendar and the other according to the Gregorian calendar. I have three, including two actual birthdays, February 18 (Gregorian calendar) and January 15 (Lunar calendar), as well as an official birthday, February 20.

What follows is the account of a series of accidents, some strange and others prosaic, which shaped my life. It is the story of a Taiwanese native born during Japanese rule, who fell into a career with the Canadian government that sent him across the world. All of it built on accidents.

Yun-Chong Pan
Toronto, Canada
August 2010

TABLE OF CONTENTS

1

BEGINNINGS

· ·

When I was ten years old, a bomb fell near my family's home in Taiwan. It happened toward the end of the war in the spring of 1945, when the allied bombing of Taiwan had intensified. I remember my father decided that our family should leave the city and the Japanese military and industrial targets of the big American B-24 bombers. We moved to the town of Diong-ho, a rural backwater in those days, and settled in a house without running water or electricity. Somehow, my father managed to get electricity connected to our new house, which made our landlord very happy. There was no school, and out of sheer boredom I picked up some of the books my parents had brought with them. I began with four classics of Chinese fictions, *Romance of the Three Kingdoms*, *Journey to the West*, *The Water Margin*, and *Dream of the Red Chamber*, which I read in Japanese translation, having been born and raised in Japanese occupied Taiwan. With the defeat of Japanese forces that same year, the bombs that forced us to seek safety in the green countryside also eventually shook us loose from half a century of Japanese rule.

I am the first son, grandson, and great-grandson, of the Pan family, a distinguished clan, long established in the Suhlim region. Pan sons had, for generations, succeeded in passing the Imperial Examinations, thereby attaining the rank of "gentlemen." Our family had also succeeded in attaining some wealth, thus winning the respect of the local community by helping to build-up the social infrastructure and by mediating communal disputes. By the time of my great-grandfather's generation, the Pan family tree had produced eight sons with my great-grandfather being the youngest, eighth son. As the first great-grandson, the family lavished its love and attention on me. When I cried at night, my grandfather, the doyen of the clan, used to carry me on his back and recite Chinese poems to lull me into sleep. One day when I was a child of four, my grandfather was carrying me and reciting Wen Tianxiang's famous 13th century Sung Dynasty poem "Zheng Qi Ge" when he momentarily forgot the next verse. I piped in and continued the poem for him dazzling him and the entire family with a little show of my early intellectual prowess. That day

I was proclaimed as the long awaited genius son that would bring the Pan clan even greater fame and wealth.

From the beginning, the omens for my place in the history of the Pan family were very clear. My mother gave birth to me early, on February 18, 1935 during the auspicious Lantern Festival that celebrated the first full moon of the Chinese lunar calendar. The city streets were brightly festooned with colorful paper lanterns and celebratory crowds went from shop to shop to socialize and flirt, solve riddles and win prizes. And while the people in the streets of Taipei celebrated under the full moon, my mother delivered me bottom-first, unlike most babies, which is another good omen. And even though I emerged from the womb with my umbilical cord around my neck (thus surviving possible strangulation at birth), I was a healthy son, who was born "seated, and wearing a necklace." Despite these signs, I'm afraid my family's hope that I would bring fabulous wealth and fame was sadly misplaced. I was born in a Taiwan that was under Japanese occupation, so perhaps the chrysanthemum and the sword, symbols of imperial rule, had disturbed the efficacy of the full moon and the other omens surrounding my birth.

Japan in the late 1930s and early 1940s was falling into the quagmire of its invasion of China. As if that was not bad enough, the nation was embarking on a gradual collision course with the "Western Imperialist Powers" surrounding the Japanese Empire and threatening its interests in China. These enemy powers consisted of America (with its territories in the Philippines and the Pacific Islands), Britain (colonial Hong Kong and Malaya-Singapore), France (colonial Vietnam, Laos, and Cambodia), and Holland (with its colonial territories in Indonesia.). The irony of Japan exercising its blatantly imperialistic power, colonizing Taiwan and Korea and then occupying parts of China did not seem to matter to the Japanese militarists. My idyllic life would be followed by war, military drills using bamboo sticks, mass mobilization (even of primary school pupils) to support the Japanese war effort, moving to the countryside to avoid bombing, and shortages of all kinds.

But my first ten years were happy ones spent in the loving embrace of my family. I was the eldest of five children; three sisters and one brother. Being the first son (and first grandson and great-grandson) I was spoiled. I became a little tyrant, and my parents did not exercise much control over my behaviour. Their leniency was partly due to their hierarchical view of siblings and they encouraged me to care for and discipline my younger siblings. It was also because they thought I was the most important child. I was insufferable. I would sometimes beat my younger siblings when they displeased me or disobeyed my commands. My eldest sister, Gloria Meiyang, suffered the most. She was two years my younger and had the misfortune of being my younger sibling during my most immature and tyrannical years. It breaks my heart to recall Meiyang begging me to play cards with her, promising me all the aces and kings. She never seemed to harbour any resentment, and today, her kindness makes me feel even more guilty for my mistreatment all of those many years ago.

I am separated from younger brother, Leigh Lichong, by nine years. The only instance of my cruelty towards him that I can remember was once, when I was practicing the violin and I asked him to bring me a dictionary. I told him not to throw it, because the binding was coming apart, but he threw it anyways and the dictionary flew apart. Furious, I hit Lichong on the head with my bow. I remember seeing the rosin dust fly from the bow as he cradled his head and cried. I still feigned anger, but was frightened and I regretted causing him such pain.

My second sister, Loretta Meizhi, was six years my junior. By the time she was born, I was six years old and so she escaped most of my despotic childhood. Too young for me to play with, Meizhi was less victimized by me. My third sister, Mae Meiling, was twelve years younger than me and because of the age difference between us, she also escaped my tyranny. By the time she had become an adult, I had already left for Canada, and our relationship did not resume until her arrival in Canada in 1974. When I came to Ottawa, I joined my four siblings again. I lived in the west end, they lived in the east end, and we saw each other frequently as our parents also lived with us.

* * *

As a subject of the Japanese Empire, I grew up speaking both Japanese and Taiwanese, and this peculiar position also gave me a unique Taiwanese perspective with which to view history and world events. Because of my family's connections, I was placed in an exclusive primary school that was primarily for Japanese pupils, instead of the ordinary school which most Taiwanese attended. The Japanese schools were much better equipped than their Taiwanese counterparts, with better qualified teachers, and lower teacher-student ratios. Consequently, the standard of education at my school was much better, especially with regard to Japanese language and history.

I do not remember exactly when I started to read, but it must have been when I was about five. I was in kindergarten when a classmate gave me a Japanese picture book about Kusunoki Masashige, a 14th century warrior who supported his beleaguered emperor and died in a desperate battle against opposing warlords. To my astonishment and delight, I understood the text. Kusunoki's story was perfect for the Japanese militarists who canonized the warrior saint as a paragon of bravery, loyalty and patriotism. Thus, I was accidentally launched on a life-long habit of reading by a piece of Japanese militarist propaganda.

And my discovery of the tale of Kusunoki also led to my double-life at the age of six. At school, I was taught to be a Japanese patriot even though I was perfectly aware that I was not really Japanese. My surname, Pan, was certainly not Japanese, and although my parents spoke to me in Japanese at home, my grandparents spoke only in Hoklo Taiwanese. Like most children, I was encouraged by my parents to be a good student, and to listen to my teachers. But I listened with increasing ambivalence as my teachers impressed upon us the unique position of Japan as a "divine nation," peopled by a superior race descended from gods, and led by an Emperor who was directly descended from the Sun Goddess Amaterasu. However, when I learned about the typhoon that twice destroyed the invading Mongol fleet in the 13th century, I was fascinated by their assertions that Japan was under divine protection. The power of this divine wind which the Japanese called "kamikaze" made me wish that I was also Japanese. Yet, when my Japanese classmates spoke derisively of the Taiwanese and their language, I felt a mixture of humiliation and resentment, because I knew they were referring to me and my people. It was then I felt the earliest, inchoate awakenings of my Taiwanese consciousness.

In my class there was a bully who I was very careful to avoid. He was a big boy, taller and heavier than me, and he was Japanese. I did not like to be pushed around by him, and I hated to see how obsequiously he behaved with our teachers. This was the first time I realized the truth of the saying, "a bully is a coward," one that I recall hearing many years later, from my good friend Warner Troyer. In 1965, when I was a young Taiwanese student in Canada, Troyer interviewed me for a Canadian Broadcasting Corporation (CBC) program about the arrest of Prof. Peng Mingmin in Taiwan for drafting a declaration of Taiwan's right to self-determination. I was interviewed in silhouette to preserve my anonymity because the issue of Taiwanese self-determination could provoke unwanted attention from adult ideological bullies.

Even though I was aware of my double life as a proud Taiwanese and as a subject of imperial Japan, I was pulled by things Japanese. I loved the stories and songs my teachers taught me, and to this day I still remember many of the Japanese songs from the Meiji and Taisho eras. Most of all, I remember the glorious stories of the heroes, geniuses, and saints of Japanese myth and history. But it was with my discovery of Western literature that turned me into a serious reader. I was nine years old when I stumbled upon my uncle's single volume anthology of Western literature, which covered everything from the ancient epics of Gilgamesh, Beowulf, and the Niebelungenlied to the masterpieces of Dante, Shakespeare, Goethe, Hugo, and Tolstoy. Each "masterpiece" was given a two page summary. It was a perfectly concise way for a nine-year old to acquire enough knowledge to show off his erudition. I can still remember being confused by "Faust" and "Crime and Punishment," and having nightmares after reading Edgar Allan Poe's stories and D'Annuncio's "Victory of Death."

At our country home in Diong-ho, I became a voracious reader, excited by discoveries of new tales, people, and places, and the fundamental experiences and emotions of the human condition. There were the low-brow Japanese versions of Harlequin romances that my parents tried to hide from me. I read them all. Although I vaguely understood the dialogue and I could follow the plots, the stories were a little over my head. I was nine, and I had no idea what sex was or what it meant. I never questioned where babies came from or how they were born. The romances were fascinating, but puzzling. How can a man and a woman throw away everything, go against all the forces of society and nature, and die in each other's arms just to be together? Not realizing that I really did not understand these stories, my parents, uncles, and aunts were horrified by my precocity when they heard me using some of the expressions I'd picked up from the romances, expressions such as "shojo" (virgin), "shinjuu" (double love-suicide), and "kantsu" (adultery), which I took literally as the combination of the characters "kan" meaning "depraved" or "sinister," and "tsu" meaning "communication" or "connection." What could be wrong with married men and women communicating with each other?

* * *

At the end of World War II, after the bombs stopped falling and the atomic dust had settled over Hiroshima and Nagasaki, the defeated Japanese surrendered and left Taiwan. Of course, with their withdrawal came the Chinese. I was told that now, all of a sudden, I was Chinese. This shift in nationality was confusing to a ten-year old, but somehow not really surprising, because I knew all along that I was not really Japanese. But to be the Chinese that the Japanese so despised? This was not a terribly exciting prospect. My elders felt differently. My grandfather, who was a young man of 19 when the Japanese arrived in Taiwan in 1895, was delighted and started teaching me the Chinese classics in their original texts. My mother decided that I should learn Mandarin to get ahead at school. She arranged for a tutor, a Taiwanese who had lived in China for a few years and whose students were mostly young wives and me, the only male.

On October 25, 1945 troops from the Republic of China accepted the formal surrender of Japanese military forces in Taipei. And while there was relief that the war had come to an end, differences between the Taiwanese and the Mainland Chinese remained a major obstacle to peace. It was not long before the Chinese would demonstrate their depravity and their terrible treatment only confirmed my apprehensions about them. The Taiwanese population felt a deep resentment and contempt against the Chinese. The situation grew so tense that the Taiwanese felt their new Chinese rulers were even worse than the hated Japanese, who had suddenly started to look good in comparison. We used to call the Japanese "four-legged dogs," but after the war ended we began calling the Chinese "pigs." At least the dogs guarded our homes, but the pigs just ate, shit and slept. This was the second awakening of my Taiwanese consciousness. At the end of World War II, I became aware that I was neither Japanese nor Chinese, but Taiwanese.

In the fall of 1945, I transferred to the Jit-hsin Primary School, a Taiwanese institution in Taipei. I had no choice because the Japanese

School I had previously attended - named after the first Japanese governor of Taiwan, Kabayama – had been destroyed by the Allied bombing and after VJ-Day there were no longer any Japanese schools left in Taiwan. At Jit-hsin, I met Lim Tinshiong and Charles Tsou, with whom I only associated perfunctorily at the time, but who became close friends after I entered National Taiwan University (Taida).

Lim was nicknamed Kabu (short for "Kabunsu" which referred to a fraction that had a value larger than one). He was named so because of his large head which made him appear slightly top-heavy. I noticed him on a sweltering summer day, as we stood at attention under the blistering sun on the school grounds listening to a speech. He was standing behind me grumbling about the hot weather.

He said "Murderous heat!" in Japanese under his breath.

I turned around in astonishment, for I did not expect this level of sophisticated mastery in Japanese from a Taiwanese primary school pupil. I looked at this boy who was 10 years old like me, standing there with beads of sweat dripping down his chin. After the drill, I approached him and struck up a conversation. I found out that he was not only very fluent in Japanese but also knowledgeable, worldly and funny. I had found a kindred spirit.

Kabu introduced me to Egyptian history and to the world of popular books about heroes from the dramatic and romantic periods of pre-modern Japan. He also taught me how to use a camera, and I learned all about aperture, focus, light, and composition from him. Kabu knew all about war planes and submarines, and he could effortlessly tick off their specifications. The two of us quickly became inseparable and we regarded ourselves as being far smarter than other, ignorant, ten year-olds.

Kabu was also responsible for my introduction to the notion of sex. It was in late 1946 and we had both done well in one of our exams. Our teacher told us not to slack off until the high school entrance exam in the coming summer. He said, in Japanese, "katte kabuto no o wo shimeyo" (after a victory, re-set your helmet strap). It was a well-known expression, and we thought it was trite. "Katte" meant "after victory," but it could also mean "after purchase." I mockingly thought up a pun and said "Katte saifu no o wo shimeyo" (after purchase, tighten your purse string). I was pleased with myself for coming up with such a clever play on words.

Kabu smiled, and said "katte gekkeitai no o wo shimeyo" (in victory tighten the sanitary napkin string).

His was a risqué turn of phrase, hinting at the battle between the sexes. I did not get the sexual connotation. He told me what a sanitary napkin was, and explained the phenomenon of menstruation. I was incredulous. Later, he showed me some "shunga," erotic Japanese woodblock prints depicting graphic sexual acts.

Sexuality was a scary and fascinating discovery. Although I was aware that girls were built differently from boys, I had no idea what it all meant. Now Kabu had opened Pandora's box for me and I became very awkward in the presence of girls, viewing them with a mixture of admiration and lust, as both angels and sex objects. I simultaneously dreaded and craved to be in the company of pretty girls, and since I had few opportunities to be with girls who were not cousins, I did not know how to behave in their presence. I usually ended up sounding pedantic, haughty, or indifferent by turn. There were a few occasions when pretty girls seemed to have been attracted to me, and some of them even sent encouraging signals, but I did not quite know how to respond. I'm sure my reactions turned them off. And reading classical love stories did not help because they represented a proof that I did not understand. Though many of my classmates had girlfriends, throughout my years at school and up to the end of my college years, I never had one.

I remember during college a few occasions when girls showed their interest in me, but I was just not interested in them. I learned to deal with the opposite sex naturally and easily only after college, when I started a job in 1959 and had the opportunity to work closely with many young ladies of my age group. Poor Kabu, he unwittingly contributed to 12 years of my rather awkward relationship with the opposite sex.

* * *

On February 28, 1947 the pent-up frustration and resentment against Chinese rule in Taiwan exploded in the infamous "228 incident." The spark that lit the fuse occurred when Chinese authorities beat a widow for selling contraband cigarettes after confiscating her goods and her life's savings. In the protest that followed, a bystander was shot and the crowd turned against the Chinese authorities. I had no idea what happened at first, and I continued to travel about town, oblivious to the growing rebellion. My parents were horrified and quickly confined me to the house. After the Taiwanese population rose up against the ruling Chinese, the Chinese Government under Chiang Kaishek sent in an army to suppress the rebellion. The streets were becoming dangerous as the invading Chinese Army started random and arbitrary arrests and executions on the streets. Thousands died at the hands of the Chinese army. Such savage and arbitrary cruelty was totally unfamiliar to the Taiwanese people, permanently scarring their collective psyche and forever changing the way they viewed the Chinese. No longer compatriots, the Chinese were now foreign occupiers. Gradually, my classmates and I became aware of what happened and we developed a deep hatred of the Chinese. We deliberately spoke in Japanese at school, refusing to answer in Mandarin, which had become the official language and which we could speak with ease. Here was another initiation. We became conscious of how different Taiwan was from China, and how Taiwan had gone through a very different process of modernization based on strong Japanese and Western influences. It became obvious to me that Taiwan was a distinct nation apart from China.

About this time, post-War Japan had begun reconstruction and their movies and magazines started to flood the Taiwanese market. Despite our resentment against Japan's prior colonial rule over Taiwan, our disgust for the Chinese made us look upon the Japanese more favourably in comparison. We used to say that the Japanese treated us like second rate citizens, but they were clean, efficient, and provided good governance. In contrast the Chinese also looked upon us like second rate citizens, and offered nothing but corruption and brutality. Consequently, we tolerated things Japanese much more easily than the Koreans. We spoke Japanese willingly, and we liked their movies, books, and food. We found refuge in Japanese culture and although I no longer wished I was Japanese, I envied their freedom and prosperity.

I was eleven when Kabu introduced me to the Japanese literature of the Meiji and Taisho eras. I was ready and I devoured them, venturing into the worlds of Natsume Soseki, Mori Ougai, and Akutagawa Ryunosuke among others. Kabu and I also went to all the Japanese movies, and we eagerly learned their theme songs. I got my initiation into he world of music via Japanese movie theme songs. Today they strike me as saccharine and banal, but back then for those of us who felt oppressed, they were refreshing in their openness and relative lack of inhibition. Of course, we also went to all the American movies and learned their theme songs too, at least partly as a way of learning English. To this day, I know many more American actors and actresses from the 40's, 50's, and 60's than the popular movie stars of the present.

Kabu was a major influence in my intellectual and emotional development until my early teens. In 1947, we entered the Seng Kong Middle School together, the same year of the "228 Incident," and the "White Terror" at the hands of the Chinese forces that followed. We shared in a lot of fun, but our relationship somehow never went beyond that of playmates to become real friendship. We never really shared our most intimate, private thoughts with each other, thoughts concerning our existential anxieties, career dreams, and feelings towards people, especially girls.

Compared to learning Mandarin Chinese, I found the English language very difficult. The grammar was complicated, and I struggled with the irregular verbs, verb tenses, and complex prepositions for which there were no clear rules. I learned Mandarin very easily, because it was so simple. Later, I had a hard time convincing people that Mandarin is the simplest language in the world from a grammatical point of view. It has no tense, no case, no gender, no plural, and no subjunctive. But having learned English, I derived great pleasure from English songs such as "The Last Rose of the Summer," "God Be With You," "Hark, The Heralding Angels Sing," and that old favourite, "Tipperary."

Music, language, and literature would become abiding passions of mine. During my summer vacations, I read all the books in my father's and uncles' collections. These included anthologies of western literature, western philosophy, and world history – often 100 volumes each - translated into Japanese and published in Japan for popular collections. These 100-volume issues were sold not only to universities and libraries, but also to ordinary citizens. It was a remarkable effort, reflecting the national aspiration of ordinary Japanese to learn as much as possible from the West. To that end, each work was accompanied by excellent, detailed, and helpful expose by a first-rate expert on the subject. I greatly benefited from these exposes, sometimes almost more than from reading the works themselves.

I started with literature, and then moved on to history and philosophy. I read the Japanese translations of the "original," unabridged versions of world literature, many of which were included in the anthology that I'd read when I was nine. I admired Victor Hugo's imaginative descriptions in *Les Miserables*, and I was moved by the nostalgic short stories by Alphonse Daudet. I pondered *Hamlet*, and became frustrated at the futile infatuations described in *The Sorrows of Young Werther* and Cyrano de Bergerac. Pushkin's *Captain's Daughter*, translated into Japanese verse, was astonishingly beautiful. *The Divine Comedy, Paradise Lost, Faust, Crime and Punishment*, and other heavier works were hard-going, but fortunately all these books came with the translator's or expert's expositions to help me along. By the time I graduated from high school, I had finished reading the three compendia of Western literature and history.

I also greatly enjoyed Chinese stories, but none of the characters in them struck me as someone I would like to have as a friend. Cao Cao was too ruthless; Liu Bei too hypocritical, Zhang Fei too boorish, Guan Yu too pigheaded, and Kongming was too righteous. Righteous bandits like Song Jiang were manipulative or they were simpletons like Lu Zhishen. Overall, they were too crude for my liking. Given the period when I was reading these Chinese stories, their plots and characters led me to perceive the Chinese as a giant race of devilishly smart, cultivated, selfish, insincere, scheming, vindictive, ruthless, and scary people. It would be much later, when I lived in China for three years and met genuinely nice people, that I even considered befriending a Chinese person. In middle school I met a lot of Chinese students, but I felt totally alienated from them. They belonged to a different culture, and I could plainly see that they felt no sympathy for Taiwan or the Taiwanese. My reading of the Chinese classics only confirmed my prejudice. This was the third awakening of my Taiwanese consciousness. At that early age, I felt that Taiwan should not be a part of China.

* * *

In 1949, after defeat at the hand of the Communists in the Chinese Mainland, the Kuomintang army retreated to Taiwan and took over all the schools in the country. Students and teachers alike were shut out, so we had a prolonged summer holiday, ultimately graduating from junior high school without taking exams. I entered the senior high school division of Seng Kong School in 1950. Kabu was still there, and I still liked him a great deal, but our association was not quite as frequent or intimate as before. I had moved on from romance novels and movie theme songs.

My new friends included Huang Quanzong, a boy I had known in junior high school. Huang's mother was a very close friend of my Third Aunt (my father's elder sister, who had died of leukemia in 1942). He could play beautiful classical music on the piano. The first piece that converted me into a fan of the genre was Handel's violin sonata in D, Op 1/13, which I heard at a recital competition played by a young violinist not much older than myself. I was electrified and realized that there was a beautiful, inspiring world of classical music to be explored. I quickly left the world of movie songs and bar tunes, and I even picked up my father's violin, which I went on to practice for years. Huang and his brothers had friends who possessed many 78 rpm classical music records, and they would organize impromptu "concerts," inviting friends to listen to recorded music with someone explaining the intricate subtleties of the pieces being played. My association with Huang brought me into this circle of music aficionados, most of them much older than myself, and they exposed me to all the great masters from Bach to Bruckner.

I was 15 and I was in heaven. I tried to bring Kabu into the circle, but he was not interested in classical music. Huang and I did not have much else in common. I found his outlook on life too worldly, too materialistic and cynical for me, and I suppose he found my outlook too naïve. We slowly drifted apart after our high-school. I was accepted into Taida and he wasn't, though I still attended his record concerts and started to invite him to ones that I had organized with my other friends. The last I heard of him was in 2001, when I was in Warsaw and was notified of a class reunion of Sengkong Senior High alumni that he was organizing.

Another schoolmate, Lim Chinghok, alias Fuku, had also become a closer friend in senior high-school. He and Kabu played a lot of Chinese chess, almost at professional level. They would go to night markets and win the set chess matches, and they were so successful that shopkeepers would beg them not to play, fearing it would distract customers and eat into their business. I remained a bystander. I was never very good at

Chinese chess, and I never managed to take the game very seriously. The three of us spent so much time together that our schoolmates dubbed us the "Three Musketeers." Fuku was also studious, and helped me with my homework when I could not be bothered to study very hard. Eventually, he joined me at Taida.

I was mostly a B student because I had spent my years in junior high school reading "irrelevant" books on history, philosophy and literature instead of school textbooks. To shame me into working harder at my studies, my mother pointed to the example of Tan Tokzuan, an A student from my home town of Suhlim. She never tired of telling me how she wished I would work half as hard as Tan.

"I know you will excel, I know you are as smart as Tan. Why don't you apply yourself?"

But I had other interests and wasn't interested in being a bookworm. I spent most of my time reading stuff totally unrelated to school textbooks, and only when I was not tooling around town with my buddies.

Though my mother used Tan to pressure me into studying more, I harboured no resentment towards him. We became quite close to each other, and I was surprised to discover that he actually had some admiration for my extracurricular knowledge of history, literature, and classical music. He was keen to listen to me talk about various subjects outside of the high-school curriculum. But looking back, I did not find him particularly admirable or interesting, though I liked him well enough. He was a bookworm, very studious and good at school work, but not especially compelling in any other way.

In 1954, the government introduced a process whereby the best students from provincial high schools were admitted into Taida and other colleges without requiring them to take the entrance exam. Because my class graduated in 1953, none of us were exempted from the entrance exam – not even Tan. I tested for three institutions (Taida, the Normal College, and the Institute of Public Administration) and passed them all. Tan did not make it into any of them. I felt sympathetic toward him. If only the system of exemption had been introduced a year earlier! First in our class, he would have undoubtedly entered Taida without having to write the exam. After trying and failing again the next year, Tan ended up graduating from the Normal College. We kept in touch over the years until the early 1970's, when he died of leukemia caused by exposure to benzene in his chemistry lab.

I never tired of reminding my mother how I might not have done as well had I listened to her advice. Tan might be much better at high-school studies, where the exams were limited to questions based on the standard curriculum textbooks, but the university entrance exams were a different story. One had to be prepared to deal with questions that sometimes required thinking outside of the box. My extracurricular readings might have made the difference. My mother acquiesced with my needling, because she was so happy with my success, and it didn't hurt that I made her feel proud and vindicated in the amusing sibling rivalry she had with her sister.

My cousin En-chiang was my mother's fourth sister's most favoured daughter. She went to the best girls' high-school in Taiwan, and my aunt never tired of boasting how smart she was and how well she was doing at school. My mother took it as a bit of a dig against my sloppy marks, and kept pushing me to work harder. En-chiang was one year senior to me, and she wrote the university entrance exam the year before me. She did not pass the exam. My mother, knowing my lousy marks, grimly expected that I would also fail, and humiliate her in the face of the Fourth Aunt. Now, she was in heaven. En-chiang and I had nothing to do with this harmless sibling rivalry. In fact, we always remained on good terms.

In 1953, Fuku and I entered Taida, where I met up with Charles again. Kabu, on the other hand, did not make it, and had to go to another city to attend an agricultural college. After I left for Canada in 1962, we lost contact with each other, and I learned of his death from cancer a few years after he passed away.

2

UNIVERSITY DAYS 1953 – 1957
• •

In the summer of 1953, the competition to gain admittance into the National Taiwan University was very fierce. There were over 2000 candidates in my faculty who wrote the entrance exam, and only 120 were admitted. Knowing my level of knowledge and the degree of my preparations, I was reasonably confident that I would succeed. My mother, who had always been worried about my unremarkable marks in high-school, was not so sure. When the results were broadcast over the radio - it was considered to be of national importance to announce the names of successful candidates into the only national university - I was happy, but my mother was beside herself. I was the first in my generation of almost 50 first cousins to win such an honour, and for my mother, it was a great victory. And what about Yanyan? When she failed in her first attempt at entrance exam, my mother had grimly expected me to also fail when my turn came a year later. Eventually, Yanyan did get into Taida, and my fourth Aunt would say, somewhat defensively, that she was good enough.

At Taida, my first taste of freedom was the realization that I no longer had to shave my head as was the practice in school, and I began to let my hair grow. My university schedule was only about fifteen hours of class, which gave me a lot of time to spend, at least in part, for studying. I met many fellow students who were knowledgeable and very intelligent, and this was a humbling experience. It destroyed my false notion that I was unique and the smartest. Of course I was not unique; I was one of some 120, actually 2000 if I counted all the new recruits in all faculties.

With the exception of Fuku, I slowly drifted apart from my earlier friends. I no longer shared an interest in movie music and popular historical stories with Kabu. Instead, I was getting into the world of Bach, Mozart, Beethoven and Wagner, and I was reading Shakespeare, Tolstoy, Hugo, Goethe, Cervantes, Dante, and Aristophanes. I quickly befriended students who came to Taida from out of town, the ones who lived in dormitories. Since I was from Taipei, I was not allocated a room in the dorms. I envied the dorm life, the opportunities to get to know students from different faculties and different years, and the countless evenings of interesting, witty, and funny conversations. I felt short-changed, and ended up spending so much time in the dorms that I was known as an honorary resident.

There was a shortage of text books in every subject except calculus. I learned to use the library extensively, and this also allowed me to pursue my extracurricular interests in subjects such as Greek philosophy. The library was also a place to run into students from different faculties, especially female students. The presence of female classmates was another new and startling difference between Taida and my prior educational environment. Many of my classmates met their girlfriends at the library, but I was too awkward, so I never made friends amongst the female students.

My university years were not very eventful. I had immersed myself in the worlds of history and philosophy, and I had no girlfriend to occupy my time. I was not exactly a hermit; I went to movies and parties just like most of my classmates. Still, I found myself talking more and more about history, and often sounding pedantic and aloof. The girls left me alone more or less. There were a few who showed some interest in me, but they did not interest me. Many of my classmates had girlfriends, and although I was envious, it didn't bother me too much because I had not found anyone that would make me lose my head.

I first caught the attention of Ao Jethiong by using a Japanese expression that he arrogantly assumed a student of my age would not know. Ao was five years older than me and we became friends along with Charles Tsou. Ao introduced me to some of the great tragedies of modern history, things that I had not been exposed to such as Stalin's purges and the Holocaust. I remember he showed me a book entitled *Nacht Und Nebel* ("Night and Fog") that described Auschwitz. It shocked me to my core. Like most Taiwanese youths at that time, I knew nothing of the Holocaust, and I could not imagine that the Nazis, "heroic" allies of Japan, were capable of such atrocities.

Despite his vast knowledge, even Kabu was not aware of the Holocaust. Those of us who grew up under the Japanese and the Kuomintang had gaping holes in our knowledge of world events. The Japanese did not provide any information about the atrocities of their German ally in the war, and the Chinese Kuomintang did not bother to either. We learned abut the war according to the nationalist perspectives of our authorities.

In the Japanese national consciousness, World War II was known as the "Great East Asian War," while in China, it was the "Anti-Japanese War" that was fought mainly on the Chinese Mainland. For Americans, World War II was fought in Western Europe and the Pacific, but not in China or Russia. While for the Russians, it was the "Great Patriotic War" against the Nazis and was fought in Eastern Europe and on Russian soil. Even the Sri Lankans have a special perspective. The sum total of their experience of World War II consists of one lone Japanese plane flying over Trincomalee and Colombo to drop a few bombs, and then buzz around Mountbatten's Supreme Command for the Allied Forces in Kandy-Peradeniya.

In my second year, I had to take a compulsory accounting course which I detested. I thought the course was intended for servants and I didn't even put in the minimal amount of effort. Consequently, I failed. Knowing that I could not graduate unless I passed accounting, I reluctantly took it again and this time put in some effort to pass. Even though the courses at Taida were much more interesting than in high-school, I still found them to be unimaginative and routine. Usually they consisted of the professor reading from his notes. So I put in little effort to pass the exams, and concentrated on extracurricular readings and discussions.

In my second year at university, my father went to the U.S. for a year with the Faculty of Forestry graduate school at the University of Michigan at Ann Arbor. Until his visit, the U.S. was just a foreign country that I knew from the movies, but now it became a place my father inhabited and he wrote home diligently describing the people, things, and places he encountered. He also sent photos, and at my request, some records, including the "Eroica" and "Jupiter" symphonies, and the violin concertos of Tchaikovsky and Mendelssohn. As soon as I received these gifts, I invited a few friends including Charles to listen to them.

When my father returned he brought a huge trunk full of gifts for my mother. This year-long absence was a revelation to me. His loving letters, the photos and the gifts made me realize just how much my father really loved my mother. They were faithful to each other all of their lives. It struck me that on my mother's part, her loyalty was more the result of her conservative nature than love. My mother had a demanding habit of evaluating my father's devotion, and she'd frequently complain that he did not do what a devoted husband should do to please his wife. In contrast, my father never criticized my mother. For my father, she could do no wrong. I would criticize her from time to time, saying she should take my father's love and loyalty and appreciate them gratefully and generously without complaint. She did not like this input from her son, but she was never angry with me because she knew that my intentions were good.

At university I wanted an opportunity to learn how to speak in English. I asked my classmate Lo Yauhuan, who was a Roman Catholic, to introduce me to a foreign priest who could teach me the catechism in English. He took me to Edouard Lafleche, a Jesuit priest. "Father,   I would like to learn the catechism in English."

Lafleche smiled, and knowing my object was not catechism but English, he said "So you want to learn English?"

We started a long association, and I'm sure Lafleche believed he could finish teaching the catechism in three months, at which point I would be ready for baptism into the Catholic faith. But we spent long hours discussing theology and even after two years, I had still not finished the three-month catechism course. Father Lafleche and I became good friends, and we kept up a correspondence after my graduation and military service. Shortly before my departure for Canada, Lafleche left for Macao, and our correspondence was interrupted. Years later, after I returned from Sri Lanka to join the CIDA China Desk, I found that one of my colleagues, Denis Legris, an ex-Jesuit who'd studied Chinese in Taiwan also knew Father Lafleche. I asked him whether it would be possible to find out where Father Lafleche was residing. He got on the phone and within a few minutes found that Lafleche was with the Holy Family Church of Taipei, and that he was in good health.

I was amazed, but Denis just smiled and said "We Jesuits have an information network as good as the CIA."

During my four years at Taida I did not make a single overnight trip. My only forays were hiking trips in the outskirts of Taipei. I spent my summers reading up on literature, history and philosophy, with occasional readings in economics. I was struck by the intellectual energy of Adam Smith, who I read in Japanese, and became a confirmed believer in laissez faire until later in life, when I was introduced to Keynes. One of our standard reference books in economics was Paul A. Samuelson's

Economics: An Introductory Analysis. Years later, at the University of Toronto, I encountered an article Samuelson wrote in the Economic Journal on factor-price equalization and I discovered a mistake in one of the diagrams.

I wrote to Samuelson, pointing out the mistake and said "I would appreciate it if you would enlighten me on whether I was right or not. I hold you responsible for leading me into the study of economics. I read your 'Introductory Analysis' in Japanese translation during my first year at the University of Taiwan."

He wrote back, very graciously acknowledging the mistake, and said "You are to be congratulated on your understanding of the material."

As graduation neared, the prospect of the military draft began to loom large. I hated the idea of living in a barrack as a common soldier, so I started to look for a way to fulfill the draft requirement while avoiding having to serve as a soldier. Fortunately, there was one possibility, that of serving as an interpreter. It was a desk job that would allow me to work at headquarters. I had to write an exam to qualify as an interpreter, and that turned out to be one of the best decisions I had ever made. Qualifying as an interpreter put me in a group of diverse people with very mixed backgrounds, and it provided me with the opportunity to meet people who I would never have met otherwise. This group include Eric Chan (through whom I met Tom Cummings), Cheyeh Lin, Akio Kashima, and Randy Den, with whom I have maintained life-long friendships.

In my final year, many of my classmates began applying for admission to American universities. I had no desire to leave Taiwan, so I remained a bystander to my friends' application frenzy. Then one of my classmates gave me a brochure for Yale University, and I was attracted by the language in its introductory pamphlet: "We are proud that you have selected us." I wrote to Yale and discovered the tuition was $2,500, and that was much more than I could consider, so I quickly abandoned that idea. I joined the army without any prospect of admission to any American universities.

Although I had hundreds of classmates, I only associated closely with a handful of them. Later, 45 years after graduation, I reconnected with my old classmates at a reunion, and I was surprised that quite a few of them felt closer to me than I had felt towards them. The long years had resulted in a great deal of knowledge and wisdom, but I suddenly realized after the reunion that I had missed out on their friendship earlier. I tried my best to maintain contact from then on, and found them to be genuine friends. They knew me as a young man, and fortunately for me, the older version they encountered did not strike them as too different.

I met Charles Tsou Chunchen almost at the start of my education. Although it was over a half a century ago and we were classmates together sporadically since primary school, our friendship has lasted ever since our first meeting. When we were drafted into the armed services after graduation, Charles and Henry were assigned to the navy, while I ended up at the Ministry of National Defense in Taipei. After out military service was over we parted ways and I left for Canada while they went to Japan before eventually returning to Taiwan.

Charles and I were in the same class when we entered the faculty of economics at Taida in 1953. We went to the movies together, to the American Embassy's recorded classical music concerts, which used state of the art stereo equipment, and we sampled the delicious food of the street stands of Taipei. Between lectures we were together all the time. I remember the first time we played Wagner's "Das Rheingold" which impressed him with the primordial darkness that grew out of the opening bars. He was moved by the Israeli songs sung by Hillel and Bat'ya in the records given to me by Tom Cummings who was teaching English at the Taipei American School.

Charles observed with a sigh, "There are so many wonderful songs and so much beautiful music that we don't know!"

When Tom Cummings gave me a recording of the Red Army Choir singing Russian folksongs, Charles and I listened to it with the excitement and surreptitious pleasure of tasting a forbidden fruit. We had to turn the volume down, and we closed the windows and drew the curtains because I lived next door to the son of Chiang Kai-shek, Jiang Jingguo, head of the secret police. Back then when Taiwan was a police state under the Kuomintang, it was dangerous to be connected with anything related to Communism, Russia, or Mainland China. Absurd as it may sound now, playing Russian songs could have gotten us into trouble, especially when the Red Army, the enemy, was singing those songs.

In 2000, while I was posted in Poland, I joined my Taida class of 1957 for a reunion aboard a luxury liner on an eleven-day cruise. We sailed from Venice to Greece, then Turkey, around the Northwest coast of the Black Sea and past Bulgaria, Rumania, and Ukraine, finally ending in Istanbul. During the cruise, I talked so much about Poland that some of my classmates showed an interest in visiting me. I told them to come, by all means, but come either as a group of four or less, or as a group of 30 or more. As a smaller group I could take them around the country in my car, and as a larger group I could hire a bus. Before the end of the cruise, I suggested that next year's reunion (2001) be held in Poland, and my classmates agreed. To my delight, both Henry and Charles came and we visited Krakow, Wieliczka Salt Mine, Auschwitz, and, of course, Warsaw and Zelazowa Wola, Chopin's birth place. Henry did not want to visit Auschwitz, but he said he was glad to have gone in the end. Back in Warsaw, my wife Hengching offered the 42 visitors some native Taiwanese food, which made a great impression because they had been living on Viennese, Czech, and Polish cuisine for over two weeks.

The 2000 reunion was an important one for me, but there was an earlier one that renewed my contact with a few friends from the Taida dormitories. Xie Jinzhong was a colleague from the dormitories that were reserved for students from out-of-town. Xie was an earnest student who worked hard at school and socialized mostly with his fellow dorm occupants. I was too busy with my other classmates to pay him much attention. When I met him again in Hawaii after 40 years in 1997, I was delighted to hear him address me in such intimate terms. I resolved to see him more whenever I was in Taiwan, where he had worked all his life and retired from a career as the CEO of a bank.

Lin Bozhi was also one of the dorm dwellers with whom I associated peripherally during university years, but we lost touch after he left Taiwan in 1960. We resumed contact after the reunion. During the university years, his English was much better than mine and I shared his interest in German literature. But I read the German masterpieces in their Japanese translation, while he learned to read them in their original. I admired his honesty and down-to-earth sense of humour, his warm and friendly temperament, and his generosity. He was also passionate about Taiwan, which I appreciated very much. When I went to Vancouver in early August 2006, I notified him of my trip and he drove all the way from Seattle to Vancouver just to be with me. It was deeply touching, and my children fell in love with him. It is truly precious to have a friend who knows you for over half a century, and still shows his unflagging devotion and care. I feel very comfortable in his presence, able to throw away any pretence or formality.

Zeng Dexin and I got along famously in our university years and I always I admired his nonchalance, humour, and outside the box thinking. We used to write to each other even during university days, because he lived in Pintung in southern Taiwan, some 300 miles from my home in Taipei. We lost contact after graduation and it was a real pleasure to see his face among those I met at the 1997 class reunion. After that, I never failed to contact him whenever I was in Taiwan. I was especially impressed by his observations on current affairs, and the social and cultural issues of the day.

Henry Kao Jing-an was six years older than me and he was from a family where his widowed mother struggled to support him, his older brother and sister. After high school, he had to work for six years before entering university, and he had to continue working to support himself while attending university with us. Since leaving Taiwan in 1962, I had only infrequent contact with Charles and Henry who stayed behind. After 1989, when Taiwan ceased to be a police state, I visited at least once a year and our contact resumed. After nearly thirty years of separation, the long gap had made no difference to our friendship. We immediately found ourselves on the same wavelength, with the same knowing glances, gestures, and jokes.

Henry and Charles had become very successful in business, and over the years Charles had taken Henry on cruises, to golf tournaments in Hokkaido, and to other fun and entertaining events. But as the younger friend, Charles always felt he owed him something.

In 2002 when I was in Warsaw, Charles wrote, "Henry died yesterday. I am at a loss. Though we knew he had cancer, I did not expect him to go so quickly. I know you share my feeling. He was a friend, and he was like the older brother I never had. And throughout my life I feel I owe him so much and yet I did not want to repay my debt to him because I was afraid that it might make me feel less grateful. Now he is gone, but my gratitude to him remains."

I cried when I read that letter because for me, Henry was also like the older brother I never had.

3

MILITARY SERVICE

. . . .

Before I could receive my Bachelor's degree from Taida, I was obliged to serve in the military for 18 months. To avoid serving combat duty, I qualified as an interpreter, translating military documents from Chinese to English and vice versa. This detail involved six extra months of service in the armed forces, making the total duration of my military service 24 months. In preparation for this service and after six months of basic training at the Infantry Academy, I had to enroll in a three-month training course on English military terms at the Officers' Language School near Taipei. But serving as an interpreter would also provide NT $400 per month of extra allowance, which was decent remuneration when one considered the average starting salary of a college graduate was only about NT $1,000. Given that I had no job prospects at the time of graduation, it was not a bad decision. Military service shielded me temporarily from worldly pressures, and it spared me from typically adult obligations such as searching for a job, finding a wife, and starting a family. It was like a nice extension of my carefree student days when there was no anxiety that failure to land a decent job would result in embarrassment and disappointment, not to mention financial difficulty.

On my first day of enlistment, I joined a group of men on a train traveling from Taipei to Fengshan in southern Taiwan. When we arrived, I was taken to the No. 10 Platoon barracks, where I was issued two sets of underwear, two sets of uniforms, a wooden stool, a wash basin, a towel, and a bar of low quality soap. My next stop was at the barber where I was lined up behind those who arrived earlier until it was my turn to have all of my hair cut off. Now I felt naked and I no longer looked like a college student. Instantly, I had lost my identity and any sense of context in this world. It was a bit depressing. The next day we were rounded up and made to sit on those little wooden stools we'd received for our initiation. Our platoon consisted of men who qualified as interpreters. Of the approximately 90 recruits, two were Taida Economics classmates, and the rest were from different faculties of Taida and a few from other colleges.

The initiation was somewhat Orwellian. We were told that all orders must be obeyed, and that we were not allowed to ask questions. If we failed to obey or to carry out our orders, no reason or excuse would be acceptable. There was no chance to ask questions after each presentation.

Finally, one of the recruits (whom I later learned was Eric Chan) asked: "What if we do not understand the meaning of the orders? Can we ask questions to clarify?"

The instructor was taken aback, and after a moment of hesitation, he said, "Yes."

We were instructed to introduce ourselves, and I felt more comfortable because the recruits' individuality started to come through as they took turns standing and introducing themselves. The Taida graduates were impressive and spoke with considerable substance.

I said that I loved to read history and literature, and that I was in awe of the great minds. The thing about the great minds, I said, was that they pursued learning by asking questions. In fact the Chinese word for learning, "xuewen" had two parts: "xue," meaning learning; and "wen," meaning inquiry, and this can be translated as "learn by asking questions," or "learn how to ask questions." It was a veiled dig at the earlier briefing.

Eric Chan introduced himself as a chemical engineer who enjoyed science and philosophy, and who valued inquisitiveness. I had never met him before, but I thought that he was very courageous for asking the question about asking questions during the lecture on the importance of blind obedience. After the initiation, I struck up a conversation with him and began a friendship that would last to this day. Over time, he proved to be a compassionate and understanding friend, as well as a source of intellectual stimulation and inspiration.

Among other things, Eric introduced me to the Mentor Books, a publisher that provided low-price paperbacks of first-class intellectual works. I had learned English well, but I never picked up the habit of reading English books in their original language. The Western books I read were all in Japanese translation, though I did read English language magazines and papers such as Time, Newsweek, and the New York Times to name a few. Thanks to Eric, I was launched into the habit of reading in English and eventually, later, in French.

Eric and I would meet every evening to discuss everything under the sun during the two hours of free time we were allotted after supper. We were young and brash, and we were intellectually fearless. We were soon joined by a few others, like Cheyeh Lin, Randy Den, Deng Renshou, Akio, Zhang Mingxiong, and Cho Meiyu. Eric introduced me to the concept of entropy as it relates to chaos, and gave me books by Alfred North Whitehead, and Arnold Toynbee, J. Robert Oppenheimer, Oswald Spengler, and others. We started a collection of pirated records and played them at our famous after-supper gatherings.

As the music played, we also discussed independence for Taiwan, an idea that could land us in jail with the prospect of torture or worse if the authorities ever discovered our conversations. We talked about the old, rebellious Kuomintang member Lei Zhen who argued that the Kuomintang should open up the political arena for free competition. Sure enough, Lei had been arrested and sentenced to ten years' in prison for sedition. We concluded that the Kuomintang was not open to discussion and had to be overthrown by force. Given that they were in control of the army, the police, and the government apparatus, we agonized on the method of how to overthrow them. We considered approaching the American government to persuade them to support us in our cause. We considered trying to cultivate relationships with American journalists, scholars, and officials to discuss the importance of supporting a grassroots independence movement in Taiwan. And we began to implement our plan as soon as we left the basic training camp and were transferred to the Officers' Language School.

My initial, brief encounter with Eric was providential. Without the military draft, he would have been a complete stranger to me, but our nine months together cemented our friendship. After we left the services, his career path and mine went in completely different directions and we stayed in touch only because we made a deliberate effort to do so and to meet whenever we had the opportunity over the next forty years.

During our six months of basic training, we largely ignored the instructions on military techniques, but we had no problem passing the tests with minimal effort. Consequently, we held a very low opinion of the military, and we became afraid for our security as it appeared that the critical matter of national defence was left to these dimwits.

We tried our best to amuse ourselves. I remember being asked to present my views on the lecture that was just given on "Sanminzhuyi," the "Three People's Principles," Kuomintang dogma written by Sun Yatsen. The lecture consisted of several points, and I was the last to be asked.

I stood up and said, "I agree with the points raised by previous speakers, but in my view, the most important point is the last principle, 'Dengdeng' because it is the broadest and most comprehensive point, and it includes everything under the sun."

Giggles broke out among the recruits and after the session, one of the mainlanders came to me, still laughing, and said "That was the damnedest joke I have ever heard."

During our training we learned that the Russians had launched Sputnik, the first space satellite. The Kuomintang leadership was in a panic because they believed their ally, the U.S., was lagging behind the Soviet Union. They were worried that their own security was now in jeopardy. To cover up this anxiety, the Kuomintang tried to downplay the significance of the event. In our training camp, we were told that this was the work of captured German scientists who had to work on something for their Soviet captors, but did not want to do anything immediately useful and applicable for terrestrial warfare. Sputnik, we were told, was just a toy in the sky. It was a lame argument. We all knew that to launch a satellite required an entire array of scientific research and development, deep knowledge of metallurgy, fuel, propulsion, guidance systems, and engineering, and that the military implications were very serious. A few months later the American satellite was launched, and the Kuomintang was so happy, they acted as if they had been responsible for the launch.

During those first six months, there was a crisis over the off-shore islands of Quemoi, when the Chinese started artillery bombardment. One of the conscripts who had been assigned to the Navy was killed during the exchange, and there was a special session to discuss the incident. Following customary protocol, there was a period for questions and comments at the end of the session.

One of our fellow conscripts in another platoon raised his hand and said: "Our Great President Chiang Kaishek said 'when one is not afraid of death, one would live.' Well, our fellow soldier died, so he must have been afraid of death."

The Chinese instructors and drill sergeant were constantly annoyed when we spoke in Japanese because they hated Japan for its invasion and occupation of China during World War II. We were amused by this and persisted in irritating them until they announced that speaking Japanese would be punished by withholding furlough privileges. So we shifted to English, which they again forbade. One of our fellow conscripts majored in Spanish, and we learned a few words of that too. Finally, frustrated by our clever pranks, we were forbidden from speaking in any foreign language.

The drill sergeants walked around the room during lectures and confiscated the books we surreptitiously read during their boring presentations. Since everyone in our platoon was a prospective interpreter, many of the books were in English or other foreign languages. I had three books confiscated, two in Japanese and one in English. The prohibition extended to nap time, when everyone was supposed to sleep between 12:30 and 1:30. On one occasion, I was reading Xunzi, a Chinese classic written by a philosopher from the third century B.C. on the art of warfare. The drill sergeant came over to me demanded that I hand over the book. He took one look at it and, somewhat taken aback, handed it back without saying anything. After that, he never bothered me again, perhaps because I was reading a revered Chinese classic, and not a wicked foreign book.

Every morning, breakfast consisted of a steamed bun, some vegetables and peanuts, and very watery porridge. It was hardly enough to sustain us until lunch, so Eric and I would get up early, sneak into the kitchen and steal an extra bun or two. Our quest for a supplemental breakfast was made easier because some of our fellow conscripts were appointed to KP (kitchen patrol) duties. We were all anxious for our days in basic training to come to an end, and we would count how many buns we had to eat before leaving the barracks.

After basic training at the Infantry Academy, I was sent to the Officers' Language School for three more months before being assigned a job in the Liaison Bureau of the Ministry of National Defence (where I served for another 15 months). Only seven of us were assigned to that Bureau, and the new friends I made at the Infantry Academy were assigned to different units. Eric was in the Logistics Headquarters, Tetsuya went to an Air Force base in southern Taiwan, and Randy Den and Akio went to other units. Although we were separated, we kept in touch and would get together most weekends.

It was during my term at the Liaison Bureau that Eric introduced me to Tom Cummings, an Anthropology graduate from Harvard University. Eric had a sister, Grace, who was studying at Normal College, and it was through Grace that I met Tom. Having been drafted into the U.S. army, Tom served in Japan for two years, and came to Taiwan for the Asia Foundation to teach English at the Teacher's College where Eric's sisters was enrolled. Tom had befriended many Japanese students from the Toh-hoku Dai in Sendai, Japan, and he could speak Japanese in a rather inventive way – sort of a mix of student slang. My friends from the Infantry Academy and I would often meet at Tom's place which was very convenient, as he had rented a large house and lived alone. Tom had a large collection of books and records which I borrowed from on a regular basis. He lent me an album of Irish folksongs by Burl Ives that helped me improve my English. I would play the songs again and again, and write down the words, which I can still remember to this day. I even borrowed idiomatic expressions from "Molly Malone," "The Auld Orange Flute," and "Paddy and the Whale," which I would use in my speeches and writings.

My period of my military service was relatively pleasant and carefree, so I dreaded its end. Not surprisingly, my friends expressed the same sentiment. But like so many youthful chapters, it did come to an end and after military service, I had to face the world of adult responsibilities. When I was discharged from the military service in the summer of 1959 I had no specific job prospects. My first job was with the Taiwanese representative office of the Osaka Shosen Company, a merchant marine shipping firm. It did not pay very much, only about NT $1,200 or U.S. $30 a month. Still, it was considered to be above average, and it was also somewhat prestigious to work for a foreign company. The job consisted of corresponding with the Navy and the Garrison Command to clear the ships' passage, and organize the loading and unloading of cargo. It was interesting at first, but it quickly grew monotonous. As we were not very busy, I had a lot of spare time that I spent reading and hiking with Eric and other friends from my military service days.

4

WORK AND MY WEDDING

After a few months with the Osaka Maritime Uncle Lo, the husband of my father's fourth sister, told me the Nippon Kangyo Bank was opening a branch in Taipei and would be recruiting. I had no desire to work for a bank, but I was bored at Osaka Maritime and the opportunity to work for a foreign firm rather than their Taiwanese agent appealed to me. I responded to the recruitment. In my interview, they called me "Ban-san" (Mr. Ban). I demurred, saying my surname ("Pan" in Mandarin) should be pronounced as "Han" in Japanese, just like the feudal principality under the Tokugawa Shogunate. As was my habit, I pedantically went on to tell them it was also the "han" of "Hai-han chi-ken," a famous policy in the early Meiji era that abolished feudal principalities and replaced them with prefectures, thus centralizing administrative authorities for the Imperial Government in Tokyo. I went home and told my parents what I'd said and they thought I should have been more diffident. Perhaps the Japanese would find me too abrasive. Somehow, I was selected along with three others from about 200 applicants.

When I reported to the job, I was introduced to the other successful candidates, including Eiji who had been one year my junior at Taida. Once we became colleagues at the Bank, we were together on a daily basis and I appreciated his razor sharp wit and his outlook of life, which resonated with mine. Eiji had lost his father as a young man, and this seemed to have instilled a sense of life's precariousness in him. Instead of morbidity, his sense of poetry made him appreciate the ephemeral moments of life. One of his favourite sayings was "when parting, leave before it becomes painful." He used to point out how absurd it would be, if, after a lot of sentimental embraces and tearful words of farewell, the plane or ship taking one away should develop a mechanical problem. Better if one left without all that fuss.

There were six female employees who had been recruited before the four of us were hired, two of whom were graduates of Taida. This situation delighted Eiji and I, providing us with an opportunity to learn how to interact with the opposite sex without being so awkward. I was now able to be myself around female companions. I no longer felt the need to impress people so much and somehow, others took note of my newfound confidence. Even several uncles and aunts commented to my mother that they noticed I was "maturing."

Tom was still in my circle of friends and he introduced us to a number of American journalists, scholars, and embassy officials. We used the occasion of dinners and receptions to advocate for a democratic and independent Taiwan, and I was surprised to see just how sympathetic these Americans were to our cause. Still, they made it clear that change could not be introduced by America, but had to come from the Taiwanese themselves. Once the Taiwanese took power, it would not be too difficult to get the U.S. to recognize Taiwan as an independent nation. Of course, this was in 1958, long before the 1972 Shanghai Communiqué issued by Nixon in China that ushered in American recognition of the People's Republic of China. We could not find fault with their argument that change must come from within, so we began trying to spread the idea that Taiwan should exist as an independent democracy. I remember translating an excerpt of the Colon Report that described the Kuomintang as corrupt and unworthy of support. I copied articles from Foreign Affairs, the New York Times, and other American publications through hand-rolled copiers and distributed them in the Taida dormitories and other places. And I continued such activities until the day I left for Canada, although my friends and I became very wary after other friends like Tan Xiaoting were arrested.

The day that I received my first salary payment, I knew the Japanese did not consider us to be colleagues, but expendable "locals" instead. The salary was a meagre NT $1,800. Eiji and I looked at each other and said that this pittance was not acceptable. We were aware of classmates such as Randy Den, who worked for Japan Airlines and made NT $4,000 a month. Did they think we were so grateful to be hired by a Japanese bank that we would work for nothing? We went to management to protest, arguing that we had foregone the opportunity to work for domestic institutions where, though our salaries might be lower, they would assure us decent pensions and fringe benefits such as a housing allowance and monthly food supplements. Their response was perfunctory and arrogant, reflecting their double standard. We were told our salaries were commensurate with local ones, and that their employees in Japan did not receive fringe benefits. The problem was that their employees did receive higher salaries – much higher salaries than us. We told them they could not invoke a local system when setting a pay scale, and then invoke a Japanese system to deny us fringe benefits. They had to decide which system they wanted to follow.

"Either you pay us local salaries and fringe benefits, or Japanese salaries without fringe benefits."

They mumbled something about having to consult the head office, but we knew that salaries were within their discretionary authority. We felt the best course of action was to give them time to save face.

For a little while, we maintained a courteous, friendly manner while interacting with our Japanese bosses, but it left a bad taste in our mouths. It was clear they never considered us as their equals because they continued to treat us as second-class citizens, just like their colonial predecessors had. I grew increasingly angry and after a few days, I felt myself on the verge of quitting. We organized what amounted to a workers' strike. When the shutter came down at three that afternoon, we continued to work until five and then we left without finishing our work for the day. The managers panicked and they stayed behind to finish our jobs. The next day, tired and red-eyed, they asked us why we'd left. What was wrong? We replied that we'd no longer work overtime and that they would have to deal with our grievances before we returned. Management begged us to stay, and promised that they'd do what they could for us.

At the end of the year, the Bank management gave us each NT $8,000 as a bonus , which was in accordance with Japanese custom. No Taiwanese company ever gave year-end bonuses. Such a large amount surprised us, and Eiji and I realized the bonus was management's solution to the salary issue. Our salaries remained the same. It was a cheap trick, but we decided to give them more time to see whether they would address the real issue. They never did.

* * *

In the midst of my difficulties at work, the one good thing to come out of my time at the bank was that I met my future wife, Hengching. Although she had lived all her life in the alley next to mine, and she had gone to the same markets, shopped at the same stores and even used the same pedicabs, I had never met Hengching until we were introduced. Old Mr. K'u was a friend of my father who was very fond of me and wanted to fix me up with a nice, neighborhood girl. He tried several times to introduce me to young ladies from reputable families, but I was never a very keen candidate. I believed in spontaneous encounters, not formal introductions. My meeting with Hengching was different. I went out of respect for Mr. K'u, but I was immediately struck by Hengching's beautiful face, her intelligence, and her sunny disposition. Her innate intellect, her sense of proportion, and her stoicism would eventually save me from many foolish mistakes. From our first meeting, I recognized that Hengching had an aristocratic temperament and bearing. She was always comfortable with herself and to this day she has never been bothered by other people's opinion of her. Born into the Lim Bun Guan family, Hengching is the closest a woman came to being a princess in Taiwan.

We were married on December 23, 1961. Both of our families had many relatives and associates, and over a thousand people attended our wedding. Back then, there was no hotel with a banquet hall that could accommodate such a large group, so we rented a school gym and set up 120 tables for our guests. Because the Taiwanese were not allowed foreign travel at that time, we went to the east coast and the southern tip of Taiwan for our honeymoon. It was a strange feeling to have someone around me all the time, day and night, even though that person was my wife. But I didn't mind a bit - I was in a marital bliss.

Hengching's open and friendly disposition made it easy for her to get along with my parents, siblings and cousins, and my friends. But I had to get used to dealing with the Lin family and their relations, who were not only numerous, but were more formal than my own family. My father-in-law seemed to like me, in part because I was his only son-in-law who discussed Japanese and Chinese history and literature with him. I remember the first time I went to his birthday lunch when Hengching's brothers and sisters and their spouses all knelt in front of her father to wish him happy birthday. Even the venerable Koo Chenfu who was married to Hengching's cousin, knelt. I was the newest and youngest son-in-law, but I was not interested in kneeling. After all, I had never knelt before anyone, not my father, my grandfather, or anyone else. So when it came turn for Hengching and me to wish my father-in-law a happy birthday, she knelt, but I stood and bowed.

"Happy birthday, Dad. May you live hundreds of years."

To my relief, he came and shook my hand. Hengching's siblings thought I was cheeky, and one of her brothers made a few snide comments about me. As her father was leaving after lunch, we all lined up to see him off, and he waved to me to join him in his car for the ride back to his office. I knew I was in his good graces.

I continued my work for the Nippon Kangyo Bank, but after some time I became alarmed by the arrests of several of my associates. They were friends introduced to me by Tom and I'd I discussed the prospect of Taiwan's independence from the Kuomintang with them. The last straw was the arrest of Tan Shaoting, a fellow Taida student one year my senior with whom I often met to discuss Taiwanese independence. A few months later, they fired Eiji under a trumped up charge. I started to feel insecure. I contemplated leaving Taiwan to avoid possible arrest. The only way one could leave the island in those days was to go abroad as a student. I discussed it with Hengching and she supported my decision. Should I decide to leave, it was not clear how long our separation would be, and there was no assurance that she could join me. I decided to write the exam for students applying for studies overseas, and I postponed the decision of whether or not I would actually leave Taiwan.

My employment at the Japanese bank was a very prestigious job, and almost everyone I knew thought I was crazy to leave such good position and my beautiful wife to become a student again. Worse yet, they were apprehensive about my moving abroad where there were no guarantees that I would survive in a foreign system. Still, I wrote the qualifying exam and passed it. Even though I was ready to leave, I had not yet applied to any university. The Bank manager saw the list of people who passed the exam and congratulated me. He asked why I wrote the exam and whether I was happy working for the bank. I responded truthfully that I had no specific university admission, and that I wasn't sure whether I would leave. I added, somewhat ingenuously, that I wrote the exam as a fall back, and to test whether I still retained what I'd learned at university.

When I began looking at prospective universities, I soon discovered that those in the U.S. were very expensive, especially the Ivy League schools. The tuition of U.S. $3,000 struck me as outrageous. I was thoroughly discouraged until one of the bank's customers mentioned that he had a cousin who was a university student in Toronto. He offered to help me find out about the tuition. At $475 a year in tuition, the University of

Toronto was the right school for me and I was admitted into the 1962/63 academic year. The university had several students from Taiwan in the Department of Political Economy before me, however, all of them failed. So I was given a conditional admission, and was admitted as a "special student." I did not become a regular student until Christmas of 1962.

I left the bank in early October of 1962 and when I subsequently left Taiwan, Eiji came to the airport to see me off. After my marriage to Hengching, my friendship with Eiji was the next best thing to have happened to me during my years at the Nippon Kangyo Bank. Eiji and I were together for only three years, but our association lasted far beyond those days. Over the next 45 years, there were periods during which we corresponded infrequently, as I was traveling from one posting to the next. I was also somewhat afraid of getting Eiji into trouble with the Kuomintang secret police. Eiji was probably too preoccupied with his fledgling business enterprise. After 1991, when the fear of the White Terror had finally lifted, I began to return to Taiwan more frequently and with every visit, Eiji would always be the first and last face I saw on the island.

Eiji became fabulously wealthy from his successful business, and in the process he had befriended many major economic and political figures in Japan and Taiwan. I was surprised at the breadth of his contacts. In 1996, he invited me to speak at the Japan-Taiwan Forum where I was introduced to many Japanese politicians, including Taro Aso who became prime minister in 2008. Eiji and I would also work together on several projects concerning Taiwan's survival strategy, and these ventures took us to Israel twice. We also collaborated on developing a non-governmental organization to promote Taiwan's interests internationally, but it was not successful because Lee Tenghui, then president of Taiwan, lacked the perspective and foresight to see it through.

5

MOVING TO CANADA

It was late evening when I arrived in Toronto's Airport. A friendly cab driver asked me if I wanted a ride.

"No, thanks, I will walk."

He proceeded to tell me that downtown Toronto was 20 miles form the airport. I took the cab. I spent that first night at a YMCA downtown at College and Yonge streets. A client of Nippon Kangyo Bank whom I knew well had given me his cousin's phone number in Toronto. Albert Lin was a graduate student of physics, and he was expecting my call. Albert took me to a rooming house at 228 Robert St., near the University campus, where he introduced me to a handful of Taiwanese students. In those days, there were only three of them – Albert, John Wu, a Chemical Engineer, and a chemist named Maisie Lin. My arrival increased the Taiwanese student population by 33 percent!

By the time I registered and oriented myself it was already a month and a half into the semester, and I was intimidated by the sight of students pouring out of various buildings with piles of books in their arms. I believed it would be prudent to take five courses because they were taught in English. Later, I discovered the average graduate student took only three courses. My classmates thought I was out of my mind to take on such a heavy course load. At Christmas break in 1962, when my five professors said I had performed satisfactorily, I decided to drop one course.

I had been in Toronto for about two months when I met Dr. Hugh MacMillan. At first, I was not particularly keen to meet him, because I held a bias against Taiwanese Christians. I felt they spoke their native Taiwanese (Hoklo) in a curiously strange way, mimicking the awkward language of their bible that had been translated from English by foreign missionaries whose grasp of Taiwanese was less than perfect. In the past, I had chastised my Taiwanese Christian friends for being phony and ignoring their mother tongue, natural Taiwanese. I viewed the foreign missionaries with a skepticism verging on hostility because I associated this perversion of the Taiwanese language and culture with the missionaries. I was also convinced that the majority of Taiwanese Presbyterians were hypocrites. But it was almost Christmas and I was alone and bored from spending long hours at the university library, cooking, and doing mundane tasks like laundry. When Albert Lin invited me to meet a Canadian Presbyterian missionary who had just returned to Toronto after many years in Taiwan, I was happy to go along.

Dr. McMillan had lived in Taiwan for 38 years, far longer than I had. He was a Presbyterian minister who received his doctorate from the University of Edinburgh in Scotland after studying theology at Knox College in Toronto. Although I had never met Dr. McMillan in Taiwan, I was familiar with the place where he worked because of its link to the famous Canadian, Leslie MacKay, the first Presbyterian missionary in Taiwan. MacKay arrived in Taiwan in 1870, married a Taiwanese woman, and lived and worked in Taiwan for the rest of his life. He is buried there. I used to look upon his center of operations, a spacious and stately complex of Victorian bungalows occupying a prime location in downtown Taipei, with a mixture of curiosity and hostility. There was something foreign, something un-Taiwanese and alien about such affluence in the midst of the poverty that marked Taiwan at the time.

I was introduced to MacMillan after he'd returned to Toronto in December 1962 to begin his retirement. He genuinely seemed to like young people, and he showed me such friendliness that I quickly felt very comfortable in his company, despite the difference of 40 years that separated us in age. I also found that he had a youthful enthusiasm and an almost naive trust in the goodness of people. Sometimes he gave people who had clearly taken advantage of him and were known to be dishonest or insincere the benefit of the doubt. Much to my frustration, it seemed to me that he would rather misplace his trust than be cynical. Like Father Lafleche in Taipei, MacMillan was another genuine Christian.

MacMillan spoke fluent Taiwanese. We soon became good friends, and she pent more time with me than he did with his own Taiwanese Christian flock (much to their chagrin). We would get together at short notice, and have Taiwanese "beefun" rice noodles, or wine and cheese, and chat. He never preached to me, but his actions and his attitude towards people expressed those of a genuine Christian. I admired the goodness of his heart, his generosity and trust in human nature, his humility and open-mindedness. MacMillan had a sunny, friendly smiling face and infectious, mischievous eyes. He had a funny habit of inserting Taiwanese words or phrases in the middle of his English sentences, which I found quite hilarious. His long sojourn in Taiwan encompassed several difficult periods, including the war years when he was considered an enemy alien to the Japanese authorities. During World War II, a police agent was assigned to tail him. MacMillan came to recognize him, and much to the agent's initial embarrassment, he would greet him whenever their eyes made contact. But it was impossible to resist Hugh's good-natured greetings and guileless manner. Over time, the tail got used to it, and would salute Hugh "by mistake." Once, after a long, grueling walk around many villages in Hualian, eastern Taiwan, MacMillan stopped for a bowl of noodles at a roadside stand, and after noticing the agent who was trying to keep a discreet distance, MacMillan approached the man and invited him to join him in a bowl of noodles.

"The poor fellow must have been as tired and hungry as I was," he said, with a chuckle.

The Taiwanese agent was obviously embarrassed, but he joined MacMillan nevertheless. They became good friends (as good as a tail can be) and after the war, they remained friendly with each other. Maybe MacMillan even managed to convert the fellow, but I forgot to ask him about that.

* * *

I was anxious for Hengching to come and join me in Toronto. Fortunately, my father had a friend who had an associate in Vancouver who issued Hengching a formal letter of invitation, and she was able to join me on April 19, 1963. I was in the middle of final exams when Hengching arrived, so I could not take her around. Of course, I hardly knew Toronto, because my experience had been limited to the rooming house, the university, and the supermarket nearby. Fortunately, my housemate Clive's wife, Katy Keirstead (she lived on the main floor and we lived in the attic), took Hengching out and showed her downtown Toronto. She came back from this first outing, and told me there was a Chinatown not far from us. She had tried to buy a few items at a store, but she was unable to communicate with the cashier. They spoke no English and they didn't understand Hengching's Mandarin. She ended up pointing to the merchandise she wanted to buy.

In the summer of 1963, I found a job with the Department of Industrial Engineering to collect the data for a performance study of all graduate students at the University of Toronto. To my horror, I found out that the economics course was the hardest to pass. With only 18% of the candidates achieving their PhD, economics was more difficult than engineering physics.

The summer job helped ease our financial strain, but we soon felt the need to earn more money. I wrote to the Federal Government's Department of the Secretary of State to inquire about the possibility of carrying out translation work from Japanese or Chinese into English, and vice versa. To my relief, I received a positive response and was sent some Japanese scientific material to translate into English. I was happy, but the scientific terms were challenging especially since the subjects ranged widely from fish disease and forestry to stochastic models of steel fabrication and geology. I wrote to my friend Akio in Kyoto who helped by sending me dictionaries on scientific terminology. This job was not especially lucrative, but along with my scholarships, it made us just enough to get by on.

The work took me to Ottawa several times where I attended the annual Canada-Japan Ministerial Meetings, a conference on North Pacific Seals Convention. And it enabled me to travel to Calgary, Vancouver, and Montreal along with the ministers. One day I appeared in a photograph on the front page of the Toronto Globe and Mail. I could be seen in the background, behind the Japanese Finance Minister who was shaking hands with Mitchell Sharp, the Canadian Finance Minister. Mrs. Servello, a neighbour of ours asked me whether I was serving at the conference. I said yes, and she said, "I hope you get good tips."

I was encouraged to find that two of my initial contacts in Canada, Albert Lin and John Wu, were advocates of a democratic and independent Taiwan. Albert and John also received the Taiwan Chinglian (Taiwan Youth), a publication out of Tokyo written by young Taiwanese advocating independence for Taiwan. They had a correspondence with the editors of the magazine. This was very exciting for me and I started to write articles in Canadian and American newspapers and magazines about the subject, and for foreign affairs periodicals. My argument for a democratic and independent Taiwan was based on simple logic: 1) Taiwan is separate from China; 2) The people of Taiwan do not wish to belong to China;

and 3) the Taiwanese are entitled to self-determination, but were under the tyrannical rule of the Kuomintang which suppressed the people using brutal and murderous means.

My emotional basis for Taiwanese independence was also very simple. Direct experience under Kuomintang rule made the Taiwanese thoroughly disgusted and contemptuous. They were resentful of the brutality, cynicism, and corruption of the Chinese, and from their observations of mainland Chinese affairs. The Taiwanese were frightened by the ruthless brutality and disregard for human dignity evidenced by Chinese Communism. In comparison, the Chinese claim over Taiwan was based on three spurious arguments: 1) The Taiwanese are Chinese, therefore Taiwan should belong to China (a racist argument, used by Hitler to annex the Sudentenland, and one that should make Singaporeans cringe); 2) Taiwan has always been a part of China. This was historically false because Taiwan was under the Japanese from 1895 to 1945, and before that the jurisdiction was ambiguous. In addition, Taiwan has been separate from China since 1949 (but this was an irrelevant argument; after all, the 13 original American colonies did not let their connection to Britain prevent them from declaring their independence); and 3) the unification of Taiwan represented the conclusion of the Chinese civil war (a strange non-sequitur in my opinion).

Strategically, it remains in the interest of the West for Taiwan to be democratic and independent. Chinese power over Taiwan would grant them open access over the Pacific. A democratic Taiwan would serve as a political beacon to the people of China, inspiring them to either reform or overthrow the Communist regime in China. If the U.S. allowed a democratic Taiwan to be taken over by China, it would destroy American credibility in the eyes of Japan and the rest of the Pacific Rim, perhaps even prompting Japan to develop nuclear arms.

I discovered articles suggesting that the Taiwanese were not ethnically Chinese because the high risk of crossing the Taiwan Strait made intermarriage between South Chinese immigrants and Taiwanese women a necessity. This argument claimed that the average Taiwanese carried less than a quarter of Chinese blood. For me, this provided a useful response to counter China's racist argument that the Taiwanese are Chinese, but I never used it as a basis for Taiwan's independence. That would be reverse-racism.

The Kuomintang's embassy in Ottawa became alarmed by the increasing activities surrounding the issue of Taiwanese independence and they sent a cultural counsellor to Toronto to investigate. At that time, there were only three or four of us writing, but we used so many pseudonyms that it gave the impression that there were dozens of writers. Although there were not many Taiwanese in Toronto at that time, there were quite a few in Ottawa and Montreal, so we decided to establish a Formosan Association of Canada (FAC). It was registered in 1963, and its founding statement declared that the FAC would be "non-profit, non-religious, and non-political." Anyone could join the FAC without being afraid of Kuomintang harassment. Of course, the idea was that a non-political banner would shield participants, while we provide a forum for intellectual and political exchange that was primarily pro-independence. The first president was Dr. Robert Y.M. Huang and later, I was elected as the third President.

Following the 228 Incident in 1947, the Kuomintang's often brutal suppression of political dissidents and communists resulted in the death and imprisonment of tens of thousands throughout the 50s and 60s in Taiwan. This period of harsh tactics under the cover of martial law was known as the "White Terror." In those days, everybody was afraid of the Kuomintang's secret police, and so for many Taiwanese even FAC's declaration of being non-political in character was not enough. I decided to ask the Kuomintang's embassy in Ottawa for financial support for one of FAC's activities - a picnic. They gave me $25. It was such a paltry and parsimonious sum that it was actually pitiful, however, it was enough for me to take advantage of this 'donation" and publicize that our activities were supported by the Kuomintang embassy. I wanted to show the Taiwanese community that there was no danger in participating in FAC activities. Over the next few years, I wrote most of the articles for publication by FAC using my real name as well as various pseudonyms.

In 1965, we expatriate Taiwanese were shocked by news of Prof. Peng Mingmin's arrest in Taiwan for drafting a declaration of Taiwan's right to self-determination. Prof. Peng Mingmin and his fellow students were charged with sedition and sentenced to eight years in prison. I was surprised, because I thought Prof. Peng was a Kuomintang protégé, as he had been favoured by the Kuomintang which had once even named him the "Young Man of the Year." Prof. Peng was a graduate of McGill

University in Montreal. As a Taiwanese living in Canada, I joined Albert Lin and Bob Huang in appealing to Prof Peng's classmates and teachers to raise objections over his arrest. I even worked with one of Prof. Peng's classmates, John Fenston, to help translate the declaration of Taiwanese self-determination.

My efforts to help Prof. Peng led me to Warner Troyer a journalist with the Canadian Broadcasting Corporation (CBC). One day the CBC called me and asked if I would be willing to appear on their program "This Hour Has Seven Days." I was wary, because I thought it could be a trap laid by the Kuomintang. I looked up the caller's name and number in the phone book and I subsequently phoned him back, agreeing to appear on the show. On the day of the interview, I was introduced to Warner who interviewed me in silhouette. The disguise did not work because the day after the interview was broadcast, I ran into Vithal Rao, one of my Indian friends, who shouted at me "Hey, TV star!" I was walking with a Chinese student, and had to discreetly ask him to quickly shut up. Finally, after all the protests by Taiwanese supporters overseas and with the interventions of Prof. Peng's colleagues and classmates, he was released after fourteen months and placed under house arrest. Prof. Peng would eventually escape to Sweden which granted him political asylum, but that happened much later.

In 1965, I received a letter from the editor of Taiwan Chinglian asking if I would be willing to accompany their chairman, K.B. Koo on a visit to Washington and New York to promote the cause of Taiwanese independence. Koo needed support because of his poor English, and I was delighted to help. I went to Washington to meet Mr. Koo and together, we met with several important U.S. senators including Wayne Morse, Frank Church, and Edward Kennedy. Some of our contacts made a poor impression and I recall William Burnett of the State Department was particularly rude and arrogant. He was obviously a Kuomintang sympathizer. In New York, we met the editor of Foreign Affairs, and Nelson Rockefeller. The visit was very useful for me because I learned first-hand the attitude of American officials. I was impressed by Senator Morse's passion for justice and democracy, and I saw that there were differences between politicians and bureaucrats.

I also got to know Mr. Koo, who told me he was impressed by my clear thinking about the issues and challenges facing Taiwan's democracy and independence. Before leaving the U.S., Mr Koo asked me to join the Taiwan Chinglian. I declined, and justified my decision by saying that they already had members in Toronto, and my joining would not add anything. I could contribute in a different way and I continued to do so in my efforts to promote Taiwan's cause. As Taiwan worked towards achieving democracy in the 90s (finally emerging from under Kuomintang rule in 2000), my effort focused on strategies for national survival.

6

WORK & FRIENDS

••

Between my University of Toronto scholarship and translating for the Federal Government, I was scraping by. A spontaneous change of routine landed me a job as an economist. I was returning home from the University, and for absolutely no reason I can remember, I turned south at Yonge Street instead of continuing on along my usual route on College. As I was walking down Yonge Street, I ran into Ivan MacPharlen, one of my classmates, as he emerged from the Dundas subway station. MacPharlen told me he was working for the Ontario Government as an economist.

I jokingly said, "Ha! If you can be an economist, so can I."

Ivan asked me if I was seriously interested in a similar position, and he referred me to the hiring committee. Curious about the job, I called, was interviewed, and offered the job.

It was not an especially challenging position. Our primary task was to write reports justifying overseas trade missions that promoted the export of goods from Ontario. It was boring, but the job provided a stable income and good contacts. I wrote these supporting documents from 1967 to 1975 – far longer than I should have stayed on. Eight years in a mediocre job illustrates the dangers of a comfortable position. I became lazy and had no interest in searching for a more challenging or satisfying job. My next position also came about by chance and in 1975 I joined the Canadian International Development Agency (CIDA).

During my work for the Ontario Government, I had the opportunity to travel to China as a member of Ontario Trade Mission. That trip was in March 1972, one week after Nixon's historic visit. In 1972 there were virtually no Taiwanese who visited China, other than those who had renounced their identity and joined the "Motherland." I wanted to take advantage of my visit. So apart from attending official functions, I also saw various points of historic interest such as the Temple of Heaven. Our host showed us the usual places like the Forbidden City, the Great Wall, the Ming Tombs, the Marco Polo Bridge, and the Huanghuagang memorial to the seventy two revolutionary martyrs of 1911. At night,

I left the Nationalities Hotel and walk along Changan Street towards Tiananmen Square. On the way to the square was the Zhongnanhai Gate, where Mao Zedong and other Communist Party leaders lived and worked. Bill Dampier, our cameraman, asked me to ask the guard whether he could take his picture.

I said, "You should ask him in English, and I will translate it for you. This would make it more natural."

The guard said no, but he didn't give us a dirty look. At Tiananmen Square we were surprised to see the entire place covered with numbers written on the cement paving stones. The numbers must have designated the location for colour plates for participants in mass rallies when they formed the giant state propaganda jigsaw puzzles.

Regardless of what I thought of China and the Chinese, the historical sites were of genuine interest and I remembered my readings in history and literature. I remember standing, contemplating the Badaling Great Wall lost in my daydreams. Arnold Bruner, a writer with our group, gently upbraided me.

I told him, "You know, for me this is like you're looking upon the Wailing Wall. Every stone speaks to me."

My words that day would come back to haunt me after John Burns, the Beijing correspondent of the Toronto Globe and Mail, published a piece about the trip and quoted my comment about the wall. I became the object of hate and ridicule by members of the "fundamentalist" Taiwan Independence faction, who attacked me for "forsaking Taiwan" and "surrendering to the Communists." Would they accuse President Kennedy of surrendering to Ireland when he said he felt at home in Ireland, or even when he said "Ich bin ein Berliner?"

There were a few things in China that I found very charming. I liked the way the native Beijingers spoke Mandarin, with their colourful colloquialisms and their curious, revolutionary vocabulary. They used the term "lover" for one's wife or husband, and I thought this was particularly accurate for its connotations of equality and non-hierarchical relations. I asked one of our hosts whether there were any significant literary works other than the official plays and ballet like "The White Haired Girl."

He said there weren't, "But we are educating the masses, and I am sure in a few years we shall have large body of literati."

I could not see that happening. Being educated is one thing; but for refined culture to develop, one needs an atmosphere of free, unfettered thought and expression.

I had expected to find strident slogans insisting on "liberating" Taiwan. But in Beijing and Guangzhou, the two cities I visited, these slogans were conspicuously absent. I had to look very hard for them and only once, in Guangzhou, did I see such sentiments on a small building off the main drag saying: "We shall definitely liberate Taiwan." I thought it was a very good sign that this sentiment was relegated to relative obscurity, but little did I know that it would persist and one day become a major policy. Today, China's aggressive approach to Taiwan is stimulated by the presence of huge Taiwanese investment and the fact that the Chinese leadership relies on "patriotism" to solidify popular support in the face of Communism's losing credibility.

I was doing well at the University and life in Toronto was good. I had developed several good friends including two Germans, Philipp Von Hahn and Aribert von Kleist. Philippe was in two of my graduate economics courses at the University of Toronto. He later introduced me to his cousin, Aribert von Kleist, with whom I subsequently developed a close friendship. I used to have lunch with Philippe, eating sandwiches at the university before Hengching came to Toronto. After her arrival in April 1963, we invited him to our rooming house for meals. One day he decided that it was his turn to invite us over for a meal. At Philippe's apartment, I noticed a Japanese monk's gown on the wall. Philippe explained that it had belonged to one of his great grand uncles who had been granted a whaling charter in the Okhotsk Sea and the Sea of Japan by Tsar Nicholas II of Russia. The great grand uncle had offices in Port Arthur and Shanghai. This was how I learned about the "Volksdeutscher" (Germans from outside of Germany) and the "Baltischer Ritterschaft," the Teutonic Knights who settled in the Baltics, Russia and Poland and then became part of the Russian aristocracy long before Catherine II was the Empress of Russia.

I met Aribert at a dinner hosted by Philipp. We had nothing in common. He was a German aristocrat. His upbringing (in Germany, Russia, Latvia, and Poland) and his experiences during World War II and in Chile were completely foreign to me. He knew very little about East Asian culture and almost nothing about Taiwan. During the war, Aribert

had been a member of the German Panzer Corp, while I was scurrying
around dodging American bombs in Taiwan. Despite our differences,
we were kindred spirits. There was a resonance in our sensibilities and
we became friends fairly quickly. Had Aribert not died suddenly in the
winter of 1990, I am sure he would have come and visited me in China,
Poland, and Ukraine. I particularly regret that he had not visited me in
Poland, where his mother had an estate before World War II and where
he'd spent part of his childhood.

Aribert's name intrigued me. I had read a few plays by Heinrich
von Kleist, who was considered the most skillful playwright in 19th
century Germany (even better than Goethe and Schiller according to
many critics). I asked him if there was any connection. Aribert said that
Heinrich was childless when he shot himself, but yes, they were distantly
related. After the meal, he offered me a plate of cheese, which I declined.

He looked at me strangely, "Don't you like it? But you eat rotten eggs,
don't you?"

I protested that the so-called "thousand-year-old eggs" were not rotten,
but processed.

"And cheese is also processed."

I obliged him and helped myself to a piece of cheese. Not long after
that evening, I invited him to our rooming house for a meal of sukiyaki.
He was taken aback to see so much soy sauce and sugar being poured
into the skillet, but once he tasted it he was hooked. I offered him a
"thousand-year-old egg" and insisted that he eat it.

"You forced me to eat your damned cheese last time."

Holding his nose, Aribert took it, and said: "The taste is not bad, but
the idea is terrible."

After that night, when he invited his friends to dinner, he would
prepare Sukiyaki and buy thousand-year old eggs to offer his guests.

Aribert was not intimidated by anyone or anything. He was not
impressed by status symbols. No amount of money, influence, position,
or titles had any effect upon him and he did not feel the need to impress
anyone. He always felt genuine happiness for his friends' good fortunes,
without the least hint of jealousy. And he was always considerate and
generous to his friends. In my life, I've only known three persons with

all of these characteristics: My wife Hengching, Aribert, and Mme. Jin Moyu, the last princess of the Manchu Dynasty.

Aribert's uncle, Cecil von Hahn, was a young aristocratic officer in the Imperial Russian Army and an aide de camp to Tsar Nicholas II during World War I. When the Prince of Wales visited Russia, Lieutenant Harold Alexander was in the Prince's entourage and Cecil befriended him. Years later, after the Russian revolution, the Hahns (and the Kleists) moved to Germany, and after World War II Cecil eventually moved to Canada. He had no money, and took a position as a laborer at Eaton's department store in Ottawa. Meanwhile, Lt. Alexander had become Field Marshall Lord Alexander of Tunis and was appointed Governor General of Canada in 1946.

After the Governor General Alexander came to Ottawa, Cecil sent him a message of greeting. The Governor General remembered his old friend and invited him to dinner. When the date of the dinner arrived, the Governor General met Cecil early so they could have more time to chat and reminisce after their years spent apart, separated by revolution and war. The Governor General went to the department store and asked for Cecil. There was a minor panic, and the store's General Manager came to receive the Governor General, but claimed not to know any Cecil Hahn. After searching around the store for a while, they found Cecil in the warehouse loading merchandise. He was summoned to the General Manager's office in his dirty work clothes. Whereupon, seeing his old friend, Lord Alexander embraced him and offered to take him to the Residence for a chat before the dinner. Cecil told him that he still had work to finish and he returned to the warehouse. He kept the Governor General waiting for another half an hour before cleaning up and joining him for dinner later that evening.

Like his older relative, Aribert would also speak his mind no matter who his interlocutor was and regardless of his status. Once the two of us were at a buffet dinner where Cheddy Jagan, the ex-prime minister of Guayana, was a guest. After praising Fidel Castro and excusing him for his executions of dissidents, Jagan began to describe how he would bring back a socialist regime to Guayana.

Aribert leaned over to me and in clearly audible whisper said, "I hope he will never succeed."

Jagan was surprised. He looked at Aribert, and was about to say something when Aribert continued, "... if people are smart!"

He told me many entertaining stories about his experiences in the Panzer Corp during World War II. For example, he was awarded an Iron Cross for shooting six Soviet tanks. During one combat mission, he noticed there was a railway track across the battlefield and that Soviet tanks were advancing across this track. Aribert saw that the Soviet tanks inadvertently exposed their undersides at the moment they crossed. He waited for the precise moment before shooting their exposed, vulnerable undersides. The tanks would flip over and explode. He managed to shoot six of them before the Soviets realized what was going on.

During another battle, he came back after the initial engagement to the rear for refitting. After he climbed out of his tank, he was expecting a pat on the back, instead he found his commander furiously pointing to his vehicle.

"Look at your tank. What the hell have you done?"

The tank was covered with white feathers. Sleeping in the open had not been comfortable, and as the tank passed an abandoned village, his team discovered several down-feather quilts, which they promptly requisitioned. They also took some tins of lard they'd found because these were a good source of energy. There was no room inside the tank, so they strapped the quilts and the tins of lard around the gun turret. In the heat of battle, they took a couple of hits and the quilts exploded along with the tins of lard. The tank looked like a giant goose.

After World War II, Germany was in ruins and Aribert, who had studied forestry at the University of Freiburg, sought greener pastures. He had to decide whether to go to an advanced country or underdeveloped country.

"Where would you go?" he asked.

I thought an underdeveloped country would be a good destination and would welcome an educated immigrant. Aribert agreed, and he had traveled to Chile, where he thought he'd be able to excel. But he soon found the Chilean socioeconomic infrastructure very unreliable, and the harder he worked, the poorer he became. In the end, he left Chile for Canada.

Aribert came to visit me when I was working for CIDA in India. Using my place as a base, he traveled all over India and was often gone for weeks at a time. He told me it took three days to travel from Katmandu to Lhasa, but only two days to return.

"Because, you see, it was all downhill coming back, and the brakes of the bus were not working."

In the winter of 1990, Aribert lost his balance and fell as he was walking down the steps of a Toronto subway station. Having survived pitched tank battles in Europe; he finally died of concussion in Canada. I was in Ottawa when I received this shocking news. His family asked me to say a few words at the funeral. I decided to speak from the heart, without prepared text. I said that when a friend dies, a part of one dies with him. I told them about the many memorable experiences we shared – picking earthworms on a golf course, fixing the valve-job on my Volkswagen, visiting Baron von Richthoven who was the cousin of the Red Baron (the famous World War I German Air Force ace), taking our families on picnics and skiing trips. One of the last stories I told the audience was when we both went to the hospital at my daughter Nadia's birth. The nurse told us that only the father of the child could see the baby.

Aribert said, "But we don't know who the father is!"

I finished my eulogy with Goethe's last line from Faust, "Alles vergaengliche ist nur ein Gleichnis (All that is ephemeral is only a metaphor). Some of his friend and family in the audience were in tears at the end of speech (including me). Afterwards, a stranger came to me and said, "When I die, if I received a eulogy like this, I would be a happy man."

7

CHILDREN

....

After two years in Canada, I was starting to feel at home in Toronto with Hengching and a number of good friends. Then, on July 3, 1964, my daughter Nadia arrived and our lives were never the same. At the time, neither Hengching nor I wanted to have children, but Nadia's arrival changed our outlook. We were inexperienced, so neither of us was alarmed by the financial pressures our baby's arrival would cause. We immediately fell in love with our baby girl. To honour the fact that she was the first Canadian born into our family, I chose to name her "Nadia" from the middle section of the word "Canadian." People would ask me why I chose this Slavic name, but my motive was entirely different. Later, when I was posted in Slavic countries like Poland and Ukraine – I would develop a deep affinity for the Slavic people, their language, folksongs, and culture – I became such a Slavophile that it's been suggested I was a Slav in my earlier incarnation. So the naming of Nadia – and later Nina – seemed at least pre-destined.

Nadia was a nervous baby who kept us up all night. Hengching did not know how to calm her and feeling powerless and frustrated, she was often reduced to tears. I suspect that our inexperience and our own nervousness might have transferred to the baby. Our friends helped us. They gave us many items that saved us a lot of money –a crib, toys, blankets, etc. We were so smitten by Nadia that our experience with her encouraged us to have more children.

I would tell Nadia, "We did not want babies, but you made us want Nina and Tom."

Nadia was a quick study. At the age of two, when she was learning to speak, she would say "I am pretty because I am Mommy's daughter," and when we told her we loved her she'd say "I love you too." Then, when she turned three, we told her that she was no longer two, but was three. One day Hengching said "I love you" and she responded "I love you three." By the time she entered Kindergarten, she had developed considerable reading skills. Once I gave her a picture with a page-long explanation and asked her to read it. After a few minutes, she gave it back to me and I said "I want you to read it." She said "I did," and proceeded to explain the text. I was dumbfounded because she appeared to be reading at three or four times my speed.

As a young girl, Nadia showed herself to be methodical and thorough. She would play with everything in the playground, one thing after another, and would not leave until she went through everything. Much later when we lived in Colombo, Sri Lanka, I arranged for the three children to take a correspondence course. Even though she was taking piano and violin classes and attending the International Children's School, Nadia prepared a chart for the course and meticulously checked the plan to ensure the coursework was up to date.

In 1967, Hengching returned to Taiwan with Nadia, who was an instant hit with our family. When she saw my mother, she introduced herself in Taiwanese, immediately captivating everyone's heart. Then she went to Hengching's home, and gave her grandfather a hug and a kiss. Hengching's father, a grand and solemn old man who had never been hugged before, let alone been kissed by a little girl, was embarrassed, but also quite charmed.

Not long after Nadia was born, we moved into a new apartment complex covered built through the Ontario Government-subsidized housing scheme. Our second daughter Nina was born there in March 19, 1968. We braced ourselves for another two years of the new baby crying all night, but were surprised when Nina remained quiet all night. She was so quiet that we worried whether she was normal or not. Of course, she would compensate for her quiet demeanour later by her enthusiastic chattiness. To prepare for the arrival of a baby sister, we attempted to deflect any sense of rivalry or sibling jealousy from Nadia. We believed we were successful in this, although perhaps the four years that separated them might also have helped.

We would probably have stayed in the Shuter Street apartment for some time had it not been for a small incident. One day in 1968, we were driving and a car blocked our way.

Nadia shouted, "Fuck off!" at the driver blocking our way.

Both Hengching and I were taken aback, as we were always careful with the words we used in her presence. We speculated that she'd picked up such bad language playing with the neighbourhood kids, and we decided to move away. The result was that in 1969 we purchased our first home at 533 Woburn Avenue, where we welcomed our son into the world on February 19, 1970.

Tom was born when I was away in Ottawa for the International Convention on North Pacific Seals, between Canada, the U.S., Japan, and the Soviet Union. While I was in Ottawa, Hengching went to the doctor for what she thought would be a routine check-up, only to learn that her uterus was dilating and that she was on the verge of giving birth. I was away, and felt totally helpless. Aribert took Hengching to the hospital. After some agonizing, Hengching, asked Jane Lin to take Nadia and Nina to their home until she was discharged from the hospital. It was all over by the time I returned to Toronto.

At home, we spoke to our children in Taiwanese because we figured they would learn English more efficiently at school than at home. Why not give them another language? At night, I told them stories from Chinese history before bedtime. I read from the original texts of the *Romance of the Western Han*, the *Romance of the Three Kingdoms*, *On the Water's Margin*, and *Journey to the West*. Initially, I unsure as to how these stories would be received, but I soon discovered that the children were captivated by the heroes, their adventures and intrigues, and the characters' scheming. Our children benefited from these stories in an unexpected way.

One day Nadia came home from her school and said, "At school they said the Chinese are ignorant and stupid, but I think they just don't know anything. The characters from the Chinese stories are so smart and so funny."

I was delighted that she had an independent mind, unaffected by stereotyping. Later, Nadia would ask me to put these stories into an English language version for children and I happily obliged her.

* * *

In August 1974, I left the Ontario Government and joined the Canadian International Development Agency (CIDA) and this meant we had to move to Ottawa. I went on alone, while Hengching stayed behind to sell the house. For the rest of that autumn and into winter, I commuted between Ottawa and Toronto, leaving Ottawa by bus on Friday afternoon, and flying back from Toronto on Monday morning. Finally, in December we sold the house and Hengching and the children joined me in the new home we bought at 257 McClellan Road in Nepean, a large suburb of Ottawa.

Family life continued peacefully, the children attended good schools and took piano lessons. Nadia had started in Toronto when she was eight years-old. She asked us to buy her a piano, and we warned her that once she started the lessons, she could not quit. Nina and Tom started even younger, when they were six, and they all continued with lessons until 1985 when we went to India. By this time, their playing ability was so advanced that they could continue learning on their own. Practicing piano was not their favourite activity, and it often involved tears of frustration. Nevertheless, they were blessed with very good teachers, Miss Archambault in Toronto, then Miss Anderson in Ottawa, and finally Miss Ellement. They became skilled enough to would participate in the annual Ottawa Piano Competitions and they won many first prizes often in age categories several years older than them.

We would live in this house for two years, but Hengching found it too large and empty, especially when I was away on mission to Afghanistan and Pakistan. In my absence, she would become frightened at night when she heard sounds downstairs. In 1977, we sold it and moved to 49 Wade Court, a semi-detached house that was much smaller and cosier. We stayed at the house on Wade Court until 1990, when we moved downtown to 191 James Street. After I retired from CIDA, we sold this, our third house, and moved to 1001 Bay St. in Toronto.

Both Nadia and Thomas graduated from University of Toronto, and Nadia went on to obtain an MBA from York University while Tom, after getting a Bachelor's in toxicology, utilized his hobby to become a computer expert and a managing director at EA, a large electronic gaming companies. Nina would turn out to be a black sheep for a few years before she finally settled in for a good, satisfying profession. Nina's university career faltered a bit, but she completed her university education and earning an M.A. in English Literature. Nina went on to obtain her teacher's certificate and ended up finding her vocation in teaching.

8

CIDA & AFGHANISTAN
....

I was ready for a change from my job in trade analysis with the Ontario Government. In the summer of 1974, Karim Durzi, a colleague of mine in the Ontario Government, directed me to a CIDA recruitment advertisement. I knew very little about the Canadian International Development Agency, but I found the idea of working there intriguing, and so with nothing to lose, I responded to the ad and was offered a job as a senior planning officer. Of course, working for CIDA meant uprooting the family, selling the house, leaving my friends in Toronto and moving to Ottawa, a much smaller town with colder and longer winters. Arnold Bruner, a fellow member of the Ontario Trade Mission to China who I met in 1972 helped me make up my mind.

He said, "You know, the bulk of your waking hours will be spent in the office. So it's job satisfaction that should determine where you want to be, not the city as such – you can always come to Toronto over the weekends."

Then he told me to close my eyes and imagine myself in Ottawa, working for CIDA. "Now, do you feel happy with your job?"

Joining CIDA in August of 1975 started me on a path that led to 16 years of overseas postings, beginning with Afghanistan and Sri Lanka (1979-82), followed by India (1985-89), China (1991-94), Poland (1998-2002), and the Ukraine (2002-04).

Bryan Wannop, who seemed to like my writing style and my way of thinking, headed my first CIDA program. I came to Ottawa alone, leaving Hengching and the children in Toronto to sell the house, and I returned to Toronto every weekend. On several weekends, Bryan had to visit Toronto. He suggested that we leave CIDA office together at noon on Friday and take the bus for Toronto, using the time to review the drafts I prepared for presentation. Bryan's company helped make the journey less dreary, and it also took me back to Toronto a few hours earlier. In December of 1975, we finally sold our house and Hengching and the children joined me in Ottawa.

For my first job, I was assigned to develop a program strategy for Afghanistan. I barely knew anything about Afghanistan, and on the third day of my joining CIDA, as I was busy reading up on the country, my boss poked his head into my office, and said: "So, you are our resident expert on Afghanistan, eh?"

Taken aback, I muttered, "Well, give me three more minutes."

In six weeks, I completed a policy draft that proposed a five-year program with enough projects to take up $4 million for its annual budget. My proposal was approved and for the first time in my life, I was on my way to Afghanistan. Before my proposal, CIDA did not have any significant projects in that part of the world, and was disbursing only $75,000 annually in Afghanistan. In 1971, this disbursement included a small scholarship that allowed the Afghan King's son to take music lessons in Montreal. Apparently, after the king was deposed by his cousin in a coup, a CIDA officer tried to inform the son, but at the time he was so drunk that he had difficulty understanding the officer's bad news.

On my way to Afghanistan, I tried to maximize the benefit of my first international trip by stopping in Rome en route to Kabul. In Rome, I had a pizza and got sick. At first, I thought the pain would go away so I tried to grin and bear it until after midnight, when it became intolerable. The English-speaking front desk clerk had gone home for the night.

In desperation, I dredged up a few Italian phrases that I knew from operas and I quoted Mozart's Cosi Fan Tutte, "Mio deo, io manco," (my God I am sick).

The clerk understood and sent for a doctor. It was winter, and the doctor placed his cold hand on my stomach as he examined me.

Quoting Puccini's La Boheme, I said "che gelida manina," (your tiny hand is cold), even though the doctor had huge hands.

He grimaced, and prepared something very black to inject into my arm. Alarmed, I said "Que cosa faccio?" (What are you doing?), also from La Boheme.

He ignored me and gave me the injection. I felt better, but after a while I could not breathe.

As the doctor was packing up to leave, I whispered, "Aspetti," (wait) from Puccini's Gianni Schicci.

He looked at me, and I quoted Mozart's Don Giovanni, "Santa Maria, Io moro," (Holy Mary, I am dying).

He waited for a while and after I had sufficiently recovered, he again prepared to leave.

I quoted once more from La Boheme, "Addio, senza rancor," (goodbye, no hard feelings).

Thank God I was not in Germany, for I would have had much more difficulty finding the appropriate phrases from Wagner.

In October 1975, I traveled to Islamabad with Bryan Wannop and drove up to Afghanistan. On the way, we passed through Peshawar, where we stayed at Dean's Hotel. Built during the British Raj, Dean's retained much of the characteristics of the period with its sprawling lawns and rich history. Former guests included Prof. Arnold Toynbee and Rudyard Kipling. Even Sir Winston Churchill had passed through Dean's as a young man on his way to Malakand. Across the street from the hotel was Hayyatt House where I bought many pieces of Raj-style furniture that I have since passed on to my children.

Driving from Islamabad to Kabul, we passed through many historically famous places including the Khyber Pass, the fabled route through which Alexander the Great came into India. When we arrived there, we were greeted by three lines of cement blocks strewn across the Pass as a tank barrier built by the British Army during World War II to block a possible German invasion. I was dumbfounded. To worry about German Panzers coming through this narrow mountain pass seemed to defy logic.

I said to Bryan, "No wonder they said that British soldiers fought like lions, but were led by donkeys."

Bryan responded that the Germans were close allies of the Afghans, and, logistical nightmares notwithstanding, who knows what they could've dreamt up? Interestingly, the Germans fondness for the Afghans was also due, in part, because Zoroaster of Friedrich Nietzsche's *Thus Spoke Zarathustra* was born in Afghanistan, along the Oxus River.

We saw Attock, where The Mughal emperor Akbar the Great had built a fortress on a strategic point overlooking the river. The narrow highway was chock- full of Pakistani trucks painted in the gaudiest manner, and they were so overloaded each truck tilted precariously to one side. Along the way, we passed many "Khyber Taxis," converted 1950's vintage Chevrolets with their trunks' covers removed to allow standing room for some dozen passengers and their luggage. They often broke down as they slowly lumbered up the Khyber Pass, but then they had the advantage of having enough muscle power to push them to the next station.

At the Pakistani-Afghan border town of Torkham, we waited for the Afghan border officials to return from their afternoon siesta and stamp our passports. As we waited, we watched as one after another, ragtag gangs of Pathans, some riding donkeys and others on camel crossing freely across the border. Apparently, the border did not exist for these people, who had been crossing back and forth for centuries. It was quite amazing that we were waiting with our diplomatic documents, while these guys on donkeys were nonchalantly passing through. I suggested that on our next visit, we should dress like Pathans and just walk through, but then what to do with our car?

As we crossed into Afghanistan, we switched to right-side driving. The highway from Torkham to Jalallabad had been built by USAID, and it was an engineering marvel with many hairpin turns through treeless crags and cliffs. As the area was seismically active, there was a constant danger of falling rocks, and after dark there was the risk of banditry. We had left Islamabad early in the morning to ensure our arrival at Kabul, or at least Jalallabad, before dusk, hoping that we would not have to wait at the border too long. Fortunately, we arrived at Jalallabad at about 3 pm, had some genuine Afghan kebabs (shashlik), and settled into the Kabul Intercontinental Hotel by about 6:30, just before sunset. The drive from Islamabad to Kabul and back, a drive that I repeated three more times, was almost a transcendental experience for me. The steepness and austerity of the barren, rocky scenery made one contemplate the harshness of nature, and the precariousness of life.

In Kabul we met with Mr. Farogh, the deputy minister of cooperation, who made us wait outside of his room for a very long and unreasonable amount of time. When he finally met us, he said rather brusquely, "Why are you here?"

It was an understandable question because CIDA had spent no more than $75,000 a year until then, and he must have wondered why CIDA would send two officers to visit such an insignificant program. This attitude changed dramatically the next year, when Bryan and I visited

Afghanistan again. I had managed to implement half a dozen major projects with a combined budget of more than $40 million over a five-year period. Apparently, this impressed Mr. Farogh who told the World Bank and other donors to emulate CIDA's effectiveness. In 1976, on our second visit to Kabul Mr. Farogh received us very warmly, and invited us to a dinner at the Bagh-i-Bala palace, where the former King had a prank chair with two flaps at the back that would suddenly close around a seated guest, covering his eyes, as a joke.

On my four visits to Afghanistan, I visited most of the famous sites including the tomb of Babur (the founder of the Mughal Dynasty) in Kabul, the White Mosque in Mazar-i-Sharif, the covered bazaar in Pur-i-Kumri, Kandahar, and the monumental Buddha statues at Bamiyan. I remember climbing the stairs behind the tallest standing statue of the Buddha in the world (which was later demolished by the Taliban in 2001). We lumbered up the stairs in the dark, and when we emerged into an open area, it turned out that we were standing on top of the Buddha's head. Not wishing to seem disrespectful, I retreated in a hurry.

I enjoyed visiting Afghanistan. I liked the food, the magnificent and austere landscape, and the very handsome people. I remember being invited to the presidential palace, where the goose-stepping guards, clad in uniforms resembling the Wehrmacht's, presented arms as we entered. I was startled to find that some of them looked very Caucasian and others very Mongoloid. But they all had one thing in common: they were very proud to be Afghans. Never having been conquered, they seemed not to harbor any chip on their shoulders.

As Canada had no embassy in Kabul at that time, our embassy in Islamabad was accredited to Afghanistan. This necessitated regular visits by embassy officers to Kabul to cover consular work. While I was visiting, there had been several consular cases. A young man had died in his cheap hotel room, and was found a few days later when the attendant came to collect payment for the room. A young woman lost her mind because her boyfriend who had brought her to Afghanistan had run away with another girl. She had to be escorted from Kabul to Islamabad by an officer so she could be re-issued a new passport and be sent home. I saw a photo of the poor girl, looking blankly in the air, propped up by an officer for the photograph. The two thumbs of the officer holding her up were visible, sticking out from her armpits, pinning her up against the wall.

I was assigned primary responsibility for Afghanistan, but my portfolio also included part of the Pakistan Program. Every time I went to Afghanistan, I also covered my projects under the Pakistan Program. As part of my work, I visited the largest earth-filled dam in the world, the Tarbella Hydro Power and Irrigation Dam in the North West Frontier Province, which measured two miles long, 1,500 feet high, and several hundred feet thick. It was so big, impounding 11 million square feet of water, that it had a significant impact on the seismic characteristics of the area. From a distance, the dam looked like a monstrous wall, with trucks running along its top like ants. I shuddered at the thought of the dam collapsing in the event of a major earthquake. It would inundate millions of acres, and kill hundreds of thousand of people.

Another interesting project was the massive Salinity Control and Reclamation Program (SCARP). Since the days of the British Raj, large-scale irrigation projects have caused the water-table to rise. Through capillary movement, the groundwater rose to the surface, carrying salt with it to the surface. After the water evaporated, the salt remained on the surface making it difficult to grow any crops. This problem was so prevalent in the provinces of Sindh and Punjab that, while flying over the land, one could see the ground covered with white salt for miles and miles. The only solution was leeching, using water to wash off the salt, and then disposing of the salty water. In order to implement this project, it was necessary to construct a huge canal system parallel to the irrigation canals to transport the saline water to the sea.

Although it was both fun and fulfilling to see these large and important projects being implemented, I had my heart set on more grassroots projects such as healthcare, polio vaccine supply, and integrated rural development programs. However, in my work in Afghanistan and Pakistan we encountered the difficult discrepancy between the government's promises and their fulfillment – a problem that is typical of so many developing countries. In our first annual Program Consultation, I mentioned to the Pakistanis that they were devoting only a tiny percentage of money to agriculture, health, and education, while their military budget was huge. I quoted the dictum of the World Bank president, Robert McNamara, that budget was the quantification of priorities. In this light, the Pakistanis should devote more to the sectors where they claimed to place their priorities. Later, Bryan Wannop told me that nobody had ever been that blunt; but that he agreed with me and was glad I'd said it.

During the four years at the Afghanistan-Pakistan desk, I rejected one project. It was a funding request for a flight simulator for Pakistan International Airlines (PIA). The simulator would cost $7 million, and with the associated infrastructure, the total cost would amount to well beyond $10 million. PIA was renting a simulator from KLM for $300 an hour. It was estimated that 12 hours of training on a simulator was required, totaling $3,600 per crewmember. If one were to train four crews of four persons each, then the total would be $59,600. At an interest rate of 10% per annum, the annual interest on the funds could train more than 60 crews for PIA, which had only one DC-10 at that time. This was the first memo I wrote to decline a request. The second would come when I was working on the China Program and I rejected a request for funding the Three Gorges Dam.

9

SRI LANKA

In the spring of 1979, Bryan Wannop, Director General of the CIDA Asia Branch, asked me if I would be interested in a posting to Sri Lanka. I was not sure I wanted it, and I didn't know then that Colombo was such a coveted post. Being inexperienced, I never had any desire for any posting, and I had no idea how a posting would affect my family. Would they be able to adapt to a completely unfamiliar environment? Bryan suggested that I go to Colombo for temporary duty while Bruce Wilson was away on holiday to see whether I liked the place.

Living in Colombo was quite pleasant, and the health and education situation was very good, especially because the Ontario Ministry of Education was offering excellent correspondence courses for primary and secondary schools. There were even excellent music instructors in Colombo for the children's piano, violin, and cello lessons. Understandably, the children were a bit afraid of being uprooted and thrown into a completely foreign environment without any friends. It took me several months of persuasion to get them to the point of resignation.

"Dad wants to go - Let's give it a try."

It was fortuitous for us that we started our posting in Sri Lanka. It was a small country, compact and easier to understand than the vast complexities of India, or the desperate poverty of African states. It was easy to travel around Sri Lanka even though the road conditions were not good for driving and it was quite a job negotiating traffic with cows, pigs, dogs, and people. Most people there understood or spoke English. I also found Sri Lanka easy to like because of its similarities with Taiwan. My background intrigued the Sri Lankans. They saw an East Asian face on a Canadian diplomat, and asked where I came from originally.

I would say that, "I was born on an island, just off shore from a continent, whose civilization we have all shared, and with which we have a love-hate relation."

"But you were not born in Sri Lanka?"

"No, I was born in Taiwan."

On our way to Colombo, we spent a week each in France and Italy. It was the first trip for our children outside of North America. In France, we drove through the Loire Valley, visiting Blois, Channonceau, Chambor and Orleans in one day, and Versailles and Chartre on the next day. In Paris, I took the children to visit the Père Lachaise cemetery, where I wanted to show them the grave of the celebrated 12th century lovers, Abelard and Heloise. We were intrigued to find a young lady kneeling in front of Chopin's grave, weeping. France met our expectations as a romantic and passionate country, as did Italy, where we packed in a quick itinerary of famous sites. In Rome we saw the Vatican, the Coliseum, the Pantheon, the Spanish Steps, and we traveled to San Pietro in Vincoli to see Michelangelo's Moses. We also ventured out by train to see the beautiful cities of Florence and Pisa.

Upon our arrival in Colombo, we first stayed in the Galle Face Hotel, the oldest Raj hotel in Sri Lanka and the model for Singapore's Ruffles Hotel. After a few days, we were moved to the Lanka Oberoi Hotel across the street and it was there, at the swimming pool that we ran into Henk Saaltink. I confess that at first, I did not think much of Henk, who was introduced to CIDA by David Veitch. A retired lieutenant colonel, Veitch was posted in India for six years, and was known to have treated his household employees as though they were orderlies in his personal army, giving them stripes on their epaulettes when he was happy with them and stripping them away when they displeased him. I was put off by his pompous and mean-spirited ways. When we were recruiting a consultant to be posted in Colombo to provide me with technical advice on the multi-sector Mahaweli Development Program, Veitch introduced Henk as someone he trusted. I assumed Henk might be the same type of person as Veitch, but I was happy to find out I couldn't have been more wrong.

Henk turned out to be a Renaissance man of broad vision, compassion, and profound wisdom. He helped prevent me from making many mistakes. Our association started professionally, but right from the beginning, I found in Henk vast knowledge and wide-ranging curiosity, a man with whom I could converse comfortably and easily. We would drive from Colombo to Maduru Oya where CIDA was financing a large dam-building project. This was a seven-hour journey by car because we could rarely drive faster than 50 kilometers per hour. We would talk during the entire trip to Maduru Oya. Henk told me later that what had previously been an exhausting drive, had become a pleasure with me, and that he was sorry that our conversation had to come to an end.

In Colombo, I inherited the big house previously occupied by my predecessor, Bruce Wilson, at 12/1 Gregory's Road, Colombo 7. It was a large, seven-bedroom house, with a big garden around it overlooking a cricket field marked off by only a low fence. We enjoyed a very luxurious life style, and the children took to it immediately. We had many dinners and receptions, often entertaining the Who's Who of Sri Lanka.

I worried that the children might find it difficult to adapt to their new lives, and that we'd have to consider placing them in boarding schools. I even briefly considered having them return to Canada with Hengching, while I stayed on to finish my posting. The children were enrolled in Colombo's Overseas Children's School, and they seemed to adapt quickly and easily to their new school and their new friends. They enjoyed school trips to different parts of Sri Lanka. Tom, who had always been afraid of water, became a good swimmer after a few lessons. Nadia, always a self-starter, completed the Ontario Ministry of Education correspondence courses while attending school as a full-time student and practicing the piano and violin everyday. Nina continued with her piano and cello lessons. Hengching visited with the ladies at the International Women's Club, and soon she had a circle of friends from all over the worlds including the U.S., U.K., Japan, Thailand, Canada, and of course, Sri Lanka.

As in all our subsequent postings, we tried to do three things in Sri Lanka: 1) Travel as much as possible both inside and outside of Sri Lanka; 2) Make as many local friends as possible; and 3) read up on the history of the country. Later, learning the language would become a fourth goal. I did not learn Sinhala because it had a limited use. However, I learned enough of it to mislead people into believing I was more fluent than I really was.

During my posting in Colombo, I took the family on as many trips as possible to Japan, Hong Kong, Singapore, Philippines, Thailand Egypt, Pakistan, India, Canada, England, and Greece. We were discovering the world together. We didn't go to these places to escape. In fact, we found Sri Lanka was one of the most undiscovered places in the world, where tourists could enjoy beautiful natural scenery, a rich historical heritage, and a very agreeable climate. We made it a point to visit most of the Buddhist sites on the island including Anuradhapura, Polonaruwa, Kandy, Kataragama, Kelaniya, Bakamunne, and spectacular beaches like Bentota, and Hikkaduwa.

* * *

One evening, as I was returning home from a reception driving along the Galle Face Green when suddenly, a man jumped out from the sidewalk into my path. To avoid hitting him, I swerved and hit a parked car. The man disappeared into the darkness, and I had to deal with the damage to the parked car. When I wrote a report on the accident, the lawyer at the CIDA Head Office suggested that I must have been driving drunk on my way back from an evening reception.

But my colleagues at the Sri Lanka Desk quickly set him straight by telling him, "No, it's impossible. Pan does not drink."

This was true, so of course I was not drunk. My reputation as a non-drinker saved the day.

I threw myself into my work and I was a very busy man. My assignment in Sri Lanka placed me in charge of all CIDA field operations in the country. My most important assignment was to oversee the implementation of the Maduru Oya Dam project, a Major Crown Project (as deemed by the Canadian Treasury Department), and the largest project CIDA had ever funded to date involving $82 million in CIDA funds.

The Maduru Oya project entailed the construction of an earth-filled dam in northeast Sri Lanka, some 350 kilometers from Colombo. The dam was part of the multi-purpose Mahaweli Development Program to direct water from the Mahaweli Ganga, Sri Lanka's largest river, for irrigation and hydroelectric power. It was such a big project that it involved all the most important multilateral donors such as the World Bank, the UNDP, the Asia Development Bank, and bilateral donors such as USAID, CIDA, German, British, Swedish, Japanese and other development agencies.

The consortium of Foundation, Atlas Gest, Fitzpatrick, and Janin (FAFJ) was awarded the contract for the actual construction of the Maduru Oya dam. In the process leading to this award, the other bidder, Marentette Brothers Ltd. (MBL) disputed the decision of the Sri Lankan

Government (based on advice that Henk, and I and the officers at CIDA had provided), and they even accused us of taking bribes to collude with FAFJ. The Audit Services Bureau sent an investigator to question us, but there was no substance to the claim. FAFJ had substantial experience in building dams, and had provided a list of specific personnel to each job post, while MBL had no dam-building experience and had provided only one name in their entire proposal. Henk and I were very cautious and we refused to meet with the representatives of FAFJ until a final official decision had been issued. Andre Jordan, the Project Manager of FAFJ, told us that while our refusal to meet him was frustrating, he did not blame us for being so careful. I remember Andre used to wear a Solidarity pin in support of Lech Walesa's movement in Gdansk, Poland. He and his wife Barbara would later visit me in Poland during my posting there in 1998 – 2002, but that was still many years away.

A fascinating development in the Maduru Oya project was the discovery of the remnants of an earlier, ancient dam over 1000 years old at the precise location that our modern engineers had identified as the best site to build our dam (with their state-of-the-art surveying equipment). The Sri Lankans were overjoyed, and wanted to preserve this ancient monument. Of course, this would mean that our dam would have to be moved some 100 meters upstream, which would cost approximately another one million dollars. Henk and I thought this extra expenditure would be worth it, as it would not only preserve an impressive monument to the skills of the ancient Sri Lankans but also promote tremendous goodwill between Canada and Sri Lanka. So I recommended that we consider increasing the budget, which was immediately approved. However, at CIDA headquarters, the enthusiasm was not quite as high.

Veitch was not happy and said, "I wish they'd make up their mind – this hassle of seeking additional funding approval is for the birds!"

His response reminded me of man I'd witnessed admiring an elaborate suit of armor on display at the Tower of London.

He turned to the man next to him and said, "Look, it's so beautiful."

"Yeah, and it's a hell of a job to clean it," said the other man who, it turned out was the man responsible for cleaning the armor.

It was not easy to manage a complex project like the Maduru Oya project, in part, because it involved several prima donnas at the CIDA

Head Office, the contractor, and the contract supervisor. CIDA hired Crippen Consulting of Vancouver as the supervisor of the contract that FAFJ was to execute, and David Martin as the project manager resident in Colombo. I quickly ran into Martin's ego.

Due to changed conditions that FAFJ claimed to be legitimate, they asked for an increase in payment in addition to the contracted amount. When I attended a meeting with the project owner (the Sri Lanka Government represented by the Mahaweli Authority), Mr. Cecil Rosa, the Additional Secretary of the Ministry of Mahaweli Development, was on the phone, and waved me to take a seat. Seated at the table were Alasdair McKee, representing FAFJ, and David Martin.

When Martin saw me, asked in a rather brusque manner, "Who invited you?"

Taken aback, I pointed to Mr. Rosa who was still on the phone.

Martin then said, "I thought the meeting was just between the owner and the contractor!"

I was livid, but I said nothing at that time. When a resolution was in sight, I decided to leave before the end of the meeting.

As I rose, I thanked Mr. Rosa and added, "As you know, CIDA is very interested in the successful execution of the project. So I would like to ask you to include me in all substantive meetings such as this, or ask Mr. Martin, who is my agent here, to notify me of the meeting."

I was fuming and told Henk Saaltink that I found Martin's behavior to be unacceptable. I considered informing my head office about it and requesting Martin's removal. Henk said he understood, but suggested that I sleep on it and decide the next morning as to the best course of action. That evening, as I relaxed in the living room with my family after dinner, the phone rang. It was Martin who asked how I was, and I responded rather icily. He told me that as he reviewed his notes from the morning's meeting, he'd noticed something unusual and asked me if I felt he was trying to push me out of the meeting. I told him it was hard to escape that impression. Then he apologized and claimed that he only asked who invited me because he'd forgotten. I knew instantly that Martin had realized his mistake and was looking for a way out. I decided to let it go rather than forcing the issue. Nothing would be gained by picking holes in his statement.

After this incident, Martin's attitude changed dramatically. He was now solicitous, and very diligent in keeping me informed of all the important developments related to the project. Overnight, he turned into a good friend. He and his wife Mae became regular fixtures at our bridge games. When I was leaving the country, he threw a very nice farewell party for us, inviting 20 people to his home, ostensibly for an evening of bridge.

When dinner was served after one rubber, as was the custom, he stood up and said, "Tonight you were invited here, not to play bridge, not to have dinner, but to say farewell to the Pan's. For the last three years, Pan has been good, professional colleague and a good friend. Now he is leaving in a few days, so I would like him to know how much we appreciate his friendship and guidance."

Then he produced a cake in the shape of a hippopotamus, and gave me a crystal hippo in the same shape. I was deeply touched. All of my friends know of my hippo collection, and over the years I have received many gifts of hippos.

My job on the Mahaweli program and the Maduru Oya project placed me in close contact with many Sri Lankan and donor officials. I particularly liked Lalit Godamunne, the Secretary General of the Mahaweli Authority. I found him to be very imaginative, flexible, and open-minded to creative suggestions. We developed an excellent rapport and eventually a personal friendship. Lalit was descended from high Kandyan aristocrats whose Godamunne Wallawwa, his family's colonial manor house, was a well-known historical site in Kandy. When I returned to Sri Lanka in 1983, a year after my departure, I asked Lorna Wright not to inform anyone, but Lalit learned of my visit and sent a car to the airport to meet me. While in Sri Lanka, Lalit gave me a car to use, despite the fact that I was no longer related to the Canadian High Commission. For 25 years after my departure from Colombo, Lalit and I would continue our correspondence with each other, and he and his wife, Preethi would come to Ottawa to stay with us several times.

I made other good friends in Sri Lanka including Warner and Glenys Troyer, a couple working on a project in Colombo. I had met Warner earlier, in 1965, when he interviewed me as a Taiwanese student, in relation to the arrest of Prof. Peng Mingmin. I remembered him, but he did not remember me. When we met, I mentioned the 1965 encounter, but Warner could not recall it.

Later, when we became more familiar with each other, he would say "but you were so forgettable."

Warner's project was to train TV producers and directors for the Rupa Vahini, the Sri Lankan national television network. It was Warner's belief that TV could be a very powerful instrument for development. He believed you could reach a large portion of the population, even the illiterate, to impart useful information and skills training. TV would also help promote democracy by informing the population of important political, economic, and social developments. I was intrigued by his idea, and it was fascinating to see how he implemented programs on nutrition, maternal health, fertilizer use, irrigation, handicraft, and the adverse effects of beetle-nut chewing.

The Troyers, especially Warner, had an unusual lifestyle. They would keep an open house and encouraged their trainees to come use their equipment and hang around. They also provided an open bar, to which I contributed (because I did not drink, I never used my quota for receptions), instead I would give my allotment of alcohol to the Troyers. Apparently, this inspired a number of rumors back at the CIDA head office.

In Ottawa, the officer in charge asked me, "Is it true that the Troyers are driving around town in embassy vehicles, consuming huge amounts of liquor, and using foul language?"

I said, "Yes. Our project does not have an editing machine, so the Troyers persuaded the Agence France Presse to allow his trainees to use their equipment. Since the AFP is located some distance away from our project office, I gave the Troyers use of vehicles that belonged to a completed project, and these are all registered under the embassy. They also keep an open house, and they let the trainees come and use the project equipment, which is kept at their house for safety. And they offer the trainees an open bar, so a lot of liquor is consumed. As for foul language, I haven't heard him use profanities, but he did say that his trainees are 'fucking good.'"

Warner's wry and self-deprecating sense of humor sometimes landed him in trouble with the Sri Lankans who did not always get his jokes.

Once, he introduced himself and Glenys saying, "Glenys and I are married, but she allows me keep my maiden name."

This did not amuse the audience, and some people even thought it was perverse. He once threw a party for trainees who were completing a course and he invited the Sri Lankan Minister of State. The Minister was a little late in arriving, and by the time he showed up, the party was in full swing. Warner wanted to call everyone's attention to the Minister's arrival, so he grabbed the nearest object to bang on the table. That object turned out to be a walrus penis bone.

"Ladies and gentlemen, I would like to announce the arrival of the Honorable Minister Anandatissa de Alwis ... by the way, you may notice the object in my hand is a walrus penis bone. The walrus is the only animal with a bone in its penis – aren't they lucky!!"

He gave the floor to the minister who was now furious and very offended by Warner's joke. In fact, he was so angry he wanted to declare Warner persona non grata. I fought hard to save the situation, including making the veiled threat of canceling the project and holding up some half a million dollars' worth of high-tech equipment. In the end, the minister relented when one of Warner's friends, Tarzi Vitachi, a Sri Lankan journalist who worked at UNICEF and was a close friend of the president of Sri Lanka, intervened.

Before we left Sri Lanka, Warner and Glenys threw a party for us and they gave me a rather unique farewell gift. After we finished dinner and the toasts were done, he rose and announced to the gathered guests,

"It is impossible to get the Pan's a suitable going away present. They were the ones who took us to shop for antique silver, gems and furniture. What can one get them? Well, as you all know this project of ours has had its ups and downs, and at times it felt like Alice in Wonderland. So, in memory of Pan's help on our project I have decided to give him this -"

He produced a carved wooden facsimile of the infamous walrus penis, mounted on a board, with a brass plate and the inscription: 'The Time Has Come, The Walrus Said.' This was the cleverest, most thoughtful present I have ever received from anyone, and I treasured it greatly. Sadly, it was lost in the process of our many moves.

* * *

With the multitude of projects scattered around Sri Lanka, I frequently had the opportunity to visit different places on the island. There was the poultry and apiculture project ("the birds and the bees project") in Kandy/ Peradeniya, a paper mill in Embilipitiya, irrigation and settlement in Anuradhapura, a fishery in Negombo, and the Katunayake international airport in Colombo. Many of the small projects all over Sri Lanka were funded under the Mission Administered Aid Fund (the MAAF, later known as the Canada Fund), which operated under CIDA's discretion. I particularly enjoyed MAAF as it gave me a chance to work with grassroots non-governmental organizations (NGOs) and I became much more familiar with the country and its people. MAAF projects also put me in contact with the wonderful people who were motivated by their desire to help others such as Brother Emmanual Nicholas (school nutrition), Father Benedict (fisheries training and marketing), and Buddhist monks from the Kiraniya Temple (vocational training). As a result of my experience with the MAAF, I would assume administration of the Canada Fund in my future postings, even though many of my colleagues thought it was too much work for such small projects.

My close contacts with other multilateral and bilateral donors provided many opportunities to enlist their cooperation on projects with Canada. For example, we needed donors for downstream development to utilize the water made available by our Maduru Oya Dam project. I was able to get USAID to take on the right bank irrigation and settlement and the Japanese to take on the left bank. Contact with other donors also made it easy for me to visit their projects and compare their work to our own. It gave me the access to use their "circuit bungalows" (guest houses for itinerant officials) when Henk and I wanted to break our long travels. Once, Hengching and I were invited by the Chinese Embassy to visit their irrigation and flood control project in Galle. It was fascinating to observe how the Chinese did their aid work. They brought everything with them, not only the machines and equipment, but also their own kitchens and cooks, drivers and laundrymen. The project even grew its own vegetables and raised its own pigs and chickens, and we were treated to the best Chinese cuisine in Sri Lanka. The food was far superior to what we found in the Chinese restaurants of Colombo. When the Japanese Ambassador was invited and a communication problem presented itself, I ended up translating for both the Chinese and the Japanese.

* * *

Whenever friends, family, or colleagues visited us, I always took them to Sigiriya, a huge rock outcropping in central Sri Lanka. Atop this massive formation, King Kasyapa built a sumptuous palace in the fifth century after killing his father and usurping his brother to claim the throne for himself. During his reign, it was said that sentries were lowered from the palace to niches carved out of the vertical rock face. These sentries guarded the King's "Rock Palace." There was standing room only for a single man in each niche, and if the sentry should doze off, then he risked falling 200 feet to his death. It was exciting to climb the rock face along the path that provided a precarious foothold. It was easier to go up than to come down, and I persuaded Hengching to ascend the path. On the way back down, she hired a man to hold her hand all the way down to the foot of the rock. She swore that this would be the last time she would follow my advice, against her own instinct. Hengching has been true to her vow. Since then, she has never joined me on cruises, or to travel to places where the facilities were not up to her standards.

The greatest aspect to every posting was the locals whom we befriended. I would often invite them to my house for dinner, and frequently I'd also invite their children, telling them that I did not want to take them away from their families. My son Thomas would put on films for their entertainment and once, when he was away, I tried to mount the film myself, unsuccessfully. There were a few engineers among the guests, and they also could not figure out how to get the projector to function. The guests clamored for my son, "We want Thomas! We want Thomas!" Fortunately, a little while later Tom came home and saved the evening.

During my three years in Sri Lanka, I had excellent access to the highest levels of the government. Sometimes I would go to a minister's office without any appointment and I was occasionally shown cabinet papers, which I read in their offices without taking notes (so a potential leak could not be attributed to my carelessness). Such access was unprecedented, and it would not to be repeated in my subsequent postings. By the time I left Colombo, I could truly say that I had met every important person in the country who was worth meeting.

As the time to leave the posting drew near, I was invited to many receptions and dinners. The most moving of these was a dinner given by the Ministry of Mahaweli Development. Nearly the entire cabinet was in attendance, including all the senior officials of the Ministry. Despite an austerity order at that time, the Ministry presented a sumptuous dinner featuring lobsters as the main course. When the time came for me to say my farewells, I rose, and embraced the Minister, the Permanent Secretary, and other senior officials. It was an emotional moment and when one of the assistant secretaries became teary-eyed, I felt deeply moved.

A week after I went back to the CIDA Head Office, a note came from the Senior VP's office asking me to go see him. When I arrived, Bill McWhinney looked at me with a long face and threw a piece of paper on the table, directing me to read it. I did not know what to expect. It was a letter that Henk Saaltink had written to Bill describing the farewell dinner in my honor by the Ministry. He wrote, "…There was a visible, but dignified demonstration of emotion. I was deeply touched, and I thought I should write to you before my memory fades."

When I finished reading the letter, Bill's long face broke into a broad smile, and he said "well done."

10

CHINA

....

After I returned from Colombo to Ottawa in July 1982, I immediately joined the newly created China Program. The staff consisted of the director, John Sinclair, and three planners, Alex Volkoff, Denis Legris, and me. Alex was a journalist who had worked in Iran, but before that she had spent two years in Beijing learning the language and fulfilling her Maoist dream of experiencing the Cultural Revolution. Denis was an ex-Jesuit who had studied in Taiwan, and we had a lot to reminisce about over our experiences in Taiwan. I told Denis about Father Lafleche, with whom I studied the Catechism for several years in Taiwan. I had lost touch with him since I left Taiwan, and I wondered whether he was still in Taiwan. Denis made a phone call and within a few minutes, he had found out Father Lafleche's address and phone number in Taiwan.

He said with a grin, "You know, the Jesuits have a network as good as the CIA."

As the senior planning officer, I assumed responsibility for the power sector and the overall planning of the China Program. In that role, I traveled to China several times and visited several planned hydroelectric project sites. It was very interesting to compare the China of 1983 to the China of 1972, when I visited the country for the first time. In 1972 Mao was still alive and China was in the middle of the brutal and destructive Cultural Revolution. Everything was grey and conformity made everyone seem like ants. A decade later, I marvelled at the emergence of an opportunistic, mercenary instinct in the Chinese.

Still, China was a society where ordinary people were separated from the privileged party members by an impassable chasm. Communism, or rather the Chinese Communist Party, did not represent egalitarianism, but a rigid hierarchical society of those in power with privileges and those under their rule. Unlike other despots in Chinese history, the Communists were much more effective in their grasp and exercise of power, leaving no room for any opposition. For one thing, the Communists brainwashed the population into believing that their suffering at the hands of foreign imperialists, the Kuomintang, and the Japanese had been perpetrated by formidable and invincible enemies who, if not for the Communists' superior ideology, strategy, and popular appeal, would have been impossible to defeat. This propaganda enabled the Communists to remain in power permanently, and although they paid lip-service to democracy, they expected the people to be content with "democracy within the party."

For Chinese communists, it was not always like this. A volume called *The Prophetic Voices from History* collates the editorials, articles, and reportage from the "pre-liberation" era and shows how the Communists argued, forcefully and brilliantly, for true democracy, multi-party politics, freedom of the press, dignity of the individual, and respect for human rights. It is a remarkable document proving that before they wrested power from the Kuomintang, the Communists had demanded all these things because they were in their interest. Of course, once they were in control everything changed and they guarded their monopoly on power fiercely. The same thing was true about Taiwan. In 1937, Mao Zedong told Edgar Snow that the Chinese Communist Party would wholeheartedly support the Korean people's struggle for freedom and independence, and "the same goes for Taiwan." But today, everything has changed.

In 1983 I joined Bill Fisher, the CIDA engineer and our technical resource, on an important mission in Guizhou. The Chinese had built an egg-shell dam, and when they discovered seismic instability in the area, a second, earth-filled gravity dam was constructed in front of the first one. The Canadian engineers had never encountered a dam site like the one at Guizhou. Initially, Bill asked me who I thought should lead the mission. As Bill was responsible for identifying and hiring consultants, I suggested he should be the team leader. Our mission began with Bill being introduced as the team leader, and he was given the official "red flag" limousine that led our motorcade. But a few days later, after many meetings in which I addressed the policy questions and the mission's details, I noticed the Chinese response to my role. Although I always deferred to Bill, I spoke on behalf of CIDA. When we arrived in Wuhan three days later, our Chinese host invited me to share the limousine with Bill.

Cost did not seem to matter in Cultural Revolution China. Near Maotai, where a famous eponymous sorghum liquor is distilled, we were treated to sumptuous dinner of armadillo meat and crispy, fried scorpions washed down with copious amounts of Maotai. The Chinese plied us with liquor by taking turns toasting us. Bill and I insisted that everyone should drink whenever one of us was asked to toast. By dinner's end, our enthusiastic hosts were all very drunk, with some of them falling off their chairs onto the floor. Bill and I remained tipsy, but upright. At the end of the evening, we supported one another, arms slung over shoulders, and stumbled our way back to our room.

Upon returning to Beijing, we were given lodging at the Xiangshan Hotel, near the Summer Palace in the northwest quarter of the city. One morning, I woke up a little early and wandered into the huge dining hall where breakfast was being served. I joined a large table where several Chinese were eating, and one of them asked me which foreign mission I was accompanying.

"The Canadian Power Sector Mission" I said.

He nodded and asked "To which ministry do you belong?"

When I told him I was the Canadian official leading the mission, his face sank, and he rose and left the table. A manager walked over and told me I was seated at the wrong table and that I should go to the foreign guests' table. I told him I'd already eaten and that I'd like to pay the bill before joining my foreign colleagues. This caused a considerable amount of confusion. The manager did no know how to deal with such an anomalous situation because foreigners were charged five or six times the price that native Chinese paid. As I had eaten at the Chinese section, the manager could not charge me the foreigner's price because the food selection was not the same. I ended up paying the Chinese rate of 90 fen, which was about fifty cents in those days.

In 1984, I went back to China on a program mission led by Don McMaster, who head of the China program at that time. On that trip, we visited Xian and Wuhan. After our official meetings in Xian, we were taken sight-seeing. Built in the Tang dynasty, the Greater Wild Goose Pagoda was famous as the location where Xuanzang, the Buddhist monk, had translated the holy Buddhist scriptures he had brought back from his travels in India. The historical record states that he died on the day he completed his translation. We saw the Huaqing Hot Springs where the imperial consort Yang Guifei, one of the "Four Beauties" of the Tang dynasty, had bathed. It was also the site of Chiang Kaishek's kidnapping in 1936 by an allied Republican general who forced him to join the communists in resisting Japanese aggression.

Of course, one of the most important historical sites in Xian was the Terracotta Army consisting of 8,000 life-size clay soldiers and hundreds of terracotta horses buried as funerary figures for the First Emperor of Qin in the third century B.C. A group of farmers who were digging a well discovered the archaeological treasure trove a decade earlier. Although this mission had turned out to be great fun, I hurt my back and was given moxibustion treatment for the first time in my life. This traditional form of medicine involves burning small amounts of ground mugwort herb near the patient's skin was a new experience for me – it did not help.

CIDA decided that we were to produce a "Five-year Country Program" document. I was the author and had to ensure that the document had the blessing of Canadian academics and NGOs. I had my first draft initially reviewed by CIDA colleagues and then by China scholars from various universities. When the final draft was reviewed by the President's Committee, their first question was, "How much did it cost?" It cost about four months of CIDA employees' time (three months of my time, plus three reviews by about ten people each, and three days of expert review involving about ten people from CIDA). I also factored in another $10,000 for the costs of five academic experts. The President was delighted because the India and Indonesia Programs had just spent more than a year's work and a million dollars on their Five-year Country Program, yet they failed to produce a satisfactory document.

In 1984, when the Chinese decided they would move forward with the construction of the massive Three Gorges Dam, they began asking for donor contributions. I wrote a memo to the cabinet recommending that Canada decline the request for a number of reasons. First, the feasibility of the project had not been established, and the dam was so large that no one could grasp the cost (estimates ranged from $20 to $60 billion). The social consequences of displacing a million people were too great. The geo-seismic implications were not clear, and the experience of Tarbela, where a large body of water caused increased seismic activity was ominous. Even the Chinese Ministry of Water Resources and Power, the agency responsible for the dam, declined to make a decision and deferred to the People's Congress, so why should a foreign government like Canada's intervene? Finally, I recommended that we should not provide Canadian taxpayers' money to finance the monumental dam, instead we should encourage the Canadian business sector to compete commercially for the project. This memo created an uproar. The Canadian consultancy sector and the equipment manufacturers wanted a piece of the action, and they wanted CIDA to pay for it. The cabinet was under intense pressure to provide funding, so against my advice, they finally decided to go forward. Subsequently, I recommended that we should fund a feasibility study, and provide the terms of reference for the study. After my departure for India, a project was approved to provide the feasibility study.

Around this time I requested an opportunity to get French language training, which was granted to me in early 1985. I made considerable progress learning French, however, by the time my posting to India was imminent, I had only reached lesson 40. According to the training center's rules, a trainee had achieved the basic level after finishing lesson 45, so I was not ready to take the test. As I had to leave in July, the center gave me the test to determine my level of French. I took the test, and received two B's for speech and listening comprehension respectively, and a C for reading. This effectively placed me above my enrolled level and I was happy to be officially classified as bilingual.

11

INDIA

By mid 1984 I was ready for another overseas posting and although the CIDA China Desk had been rewarding, I felt three years of head office work was enough. When we left my posting in Sri Lanka, I recalled that the children had been rooting for India because they had fallen in love with the country when we traveled there in 1981. Although the idea of India was appealing, I thought I should try to get a posting to Tokyo and I began to explore that possibility with the Department of Foreign Affairs. The officials there told me they were impressed by my knowledge of Japan, and I thought that they were seriously considering a posting for me in 1985. Consequently, I made the mistake of allowing the application deadline for CIDA's posting to pass without registering my name. In December 1984, I had not heard from Foreign Affairs and after I prodded them, they told me someone else had been posted to Tokyo.

Disappointed and angry, I saw Art Saper, director of the CIDA India Program, and told him that I was interested in a posting to India. He was very pleased, but a little annoyed that I had missed the application deadline. I told him what happened with my interest in Japan.

He laughed, and he said, "You know, blood is thicker than water."

Indeed, it was clear that I belonged to CIDA and not to Foreign Affairs. The CIDA posting exercise was already well into the second stage of candidate screenings, but Art managed to insert my candidacy into the process and through his efforts, I was nominated to go to Delhi in July 1985. When I announced the India posting to the family, everyone was happy. When Nina broke the news to Nadia, who then was living at Whitney Hall at the University of Toronto, I remember hearing Nadia shout with joy over the telephone.

We were immediately pleased with my new posting. The Canadian High Commission, designed by the renowned architect Arthur Erickson, was an attractive building with a solar powered swimming pool, two tennis courts, and a cabana where the children could hang out. Best of all, we had a very spacious and well-appointed home that was also fully air-conditioned – an important amenity in New Delhi where the summer temperatures were frequently above 40 degrees Celsius. We had a lot of help including a cook, a laundry man, a sweeper, a gardener, and two guards who worked two shifts. Nina and Tom attended the established American Embassy School, which had high academic standards and plenty of extracurricular activities including drama, hiking in Sikkim, white-water rafting in the Himalayas, field hockey, swimming, and diving. Tom joined the diving team, and became a bit of a star. I complained that I was never acknowledged as a person in my own right because, as a young man, I was known as my father's son, and now I was known as my children's father.

I began to learn Hindi immediately and I found the language was very logical and easier than French or English. There are only six irregular verbs in Hindi. After about a year of taking two lessons a week, I was able to converse and even make speeches. Meanwhile, I also took French lessons twice a week to maintain my proficiency. The focus on these two languages sometimes resulted in my confusing them, and I would use vocabulary from one language when speaking the other.

My job took me to many places in India and even to Bhutan. Apart from my numerous business trips, Hengching and I traveled frequently on our own time. I visited all of India's states except Punjab, which was off limits to diplomats at that time, and Sikkim, which had only become an Indian state in 1975 and was a new addition to the nation.

* * *

In India I took on the $675 million Chamera Hydro-Electric Dam project in Himachal Pradesh, the largest CIDA project to date involving $225 million of CIDA funds and $450 million of Export Development Canada (EDC) funds. Originally, I was to be dedicated exclusively to Chamera and nothing else. But I found myself able to work on other projects such as he Idduki Hydro-electric project in Kerala, one of the oldest CIDA infrastructure efforts. These were large and complex projects, but I still found myself not fully occupied, so I volunteered to take on the Canada Fund program, and occasionally offered my services for consular work.

On the Chamera Dam project The National Hydro Power Corporation of India (NHPC) was the executing agency and it had a construction contract for the Dam with Canada's SNC-Acres under a CIDA loan. CIDA hired the Montreal engineering firm of Rousseau, Sauve and Warren (RSW) with a grant to monitor the project execution. I visited Chamera about every two months, or whenever there was a mission ordered from Headquarters. The trip usually involved a train journey overnight through Haryana to Pathankot in Punjab, followed by a drive from Pathankot through the mountains of Himachal Pradesh to the town of Dalhousie. It was an arduous journey, but I was always in good company on the way up. It was a complex project that required the construction of a coffer dam, a diversion tunnel, and a main dam. Chamera involved numerous subcontracts, such as cement fabrication by Indian companies, transport of cement to the construction sites, and the construction of huge cables to pour the cement over the main dam, which was truly a spectacular sight.

CIDA recognized the need to hire a project monitor because of the Chamera project's size and complexity and was prepared to provide a grant to pay for this assignment. But NHPC felt it was unnecessary, and SNC/Acres considered it a nuisance. Bill Pearson, the VP of SNC in charge of Chamera, argued strongly against it and claimed there was enough supervision in place provided by the NHPC. I thought we needed an independent Canadian monitor to ensure work quality and timeliness. Bill's attitude encouraged the Indians to resist our request to establish a grant to pay for the monitoring service. To move past this deadlock, I decided to play on Bill Pearson's psychology. In the early stage of the project before the implementation phase began, CIDA relied on Antoine Kaiser, an independent consultant, to monitor the project. Kaiser was competent enough, but he was a very peculiar bird with strange eccentricities and a big chip on his shoulders. Bill Pearson could not stand him.

When Bill reiterated his objection to hiring a monitor, I suggested rather innocently, "I suppose, if worst comes to worst, instead of hiring a firm, we might consider asking Mr. Kaiser to monitor for the duration of the project."

Bill's face sank, and he became quiet. Subsequently, there was no more resistance from SNC, and the Indians signed the CIDA grant provision. The engineering firm of RSW fielded Allen MacConnell to head their monitoring team, with John Jutasi and a few other members. Allen turned out to be both professionally competent and politically sensitive. He served a similar role that Henk Saaltink had served for Maduru Oya in Sri Lanka, although he and I never developed such a close personal relationship as the one I shared with Henk. Allen was a little more reserved, and he did not live in Delhi, so we never had the opportunity to associate with each other outside of our work on the project.

Chamera was a Major Crown Project and as such, it attracted a lot of visitors. Once, a senior official from the Treasury Board in charge of development funding came to visit the project and I naturally accompanied her. On our way up the mountain, there was a flash flood that made it difficult to cross the riverbed which was usually dry, but was now a torrent of water. We stopped on one side of the river, waiting for the flow to subside. A bus driver who had also stopped nearby became impatient, and started to drive through the rushing water. We watched in horror as the bus was swept downstream. We waited few more hours, and when the water level was down to about one foot, I decided to take a chance and attempt a crossing. I hired ten young men who were standing around watching the drama, and showed them how to position themselves on the right side of our car. They began pushing the car against the stream as we drove. After a successful crossing, I paid them each 100 rupees. I was soaked through, so I asked my visitor to turn her head while I changed my underwear and trousers inside the car. It was almost three in the afternoon, some four hours after our scheduled time of arrival in Dalhousie.

We had not eaten lunch, so I bought a few bananas and told my guest, "If it's good enough for monkeys, it's good enough for us."

As we were nearing Dalhousie, there was a rock slide that made it impossible for us to drive on. The Chamera Project Office in Dalhousie had learned about our plight at the river and the rock slide, and had sent a car to meet us on the other side. But as the road was covered with rocks and mud, we feared another slide. I suggested that we climb above and around the rock slide to get to the other side. My guest had no choice, and after we successfully climbed to the other side, she confessed to being very frightened.

As we drove back through the high mountains of Himachal Pradesh at an altitude of some 8000 feet above sea level, I still recall how we were accompanied for a few moments by a falcon flying alongside at eye-level.

The visit turned out to be a success, and the treasury official saw how well CIDA was supervising the management of such a complex and difficult project.

In 1988, Hengching visited the Chamera Project with me, and we drove back to Delhi via Dharamsala, in order to visit the residence of the exiled Dalai Lama. Canada Fund had awarded some assistance to one of the Dalai Lama's senior assistants, Tempa Tsering, to develop a carpet-weaving training project for Tibetan refugees and local Indians. Tempa waited for us at the Tibetan compound, and led us on a tour of the Dalai Lama's hilltop residence. From the windows of his home, the revered Buddhist leader could look out over the valley and the distant, cloudy mountains of his homeland. The Dalai Lama was not there, but we saw his private apartments which were panelled in wood and decorated with many colourful paintings (*thangka*), with parquet wood flooring, beautiful silk carpets, vases filled with flowers, and many shelves full of books.

A few years later, in July 1989 I asked Rimpoche Doboom Tulku, the head of Tibet House in Delhi, to arrange an audience with the Dalai Lama. The appointment was for 15 minutes, so I had to be concise and get to the point. I told the Dalai Lama that I was a Canadian, but was born in Taiwan, and that I had great sympathy toward him and the Tibetan people. Both Taiwan and Tibet were victims of China's tyranny, although Tibet had suffered much more than Taiwan. When the meeting came to an end, I rose to thank him for giving me an opportunity to meet with him. To my surprise, he motioned for me to stay, so I sat and spoke with him for another 15 minutes. We discussed the Tiananmen Square massacre that had occurred in June of that year. I thought China was unwise in denying the massacre in the face of such extensive Western media coverage. The Dalai Lama agreed and stated that this denial showed how disconnected the Chinese leadership was from the rest of the world. They thought they could get away with what they did by denying it, not realizing that this would be considered dishonest, and an insult to the collective intelligence of humanity. When I rose again to say good bye, again he motioned for me to stay. Finally, after 45 minutes, when I stood up to say goodbye he told me to wait, and went into the next room to fetch a book and a silver Tibetan coin for me. The Dalai Lama inscribed the book in Tibetan: "To YC Pan, the object of my prayer, with best wishes. Buddhist Monk Tenzin Gyatso." I was very happy to receive this autographed book, and I was especially impressed by his humility in signing only his name, not his title.

* * *

Once, I made the entire trip to Dalhousie by car instead of train. This involved flying to Kulu and then driving to Dalhousie, some eight hours away. When I arrived at the Kulu airport, I noticed two young, blonde women looking at the Canadian High Commission car that was waiting for me. The driver said they were Canadians who lived in an ashram in Kulu. This piqued my curiosity, so I decided to find out more about them. On my way back from Dalhousie, I used the three hours I had before my flight to visit the ashram. I discovered there were about 30 Canadians who were mostly professionals including Barbara Mulroney, the sister of then Canadian Prime Minister, Brian Mulroney. Apparently, they were causing a few consular problems for the High commission, and my colleagues in the Consular Section were anxious not to have them too close. I knew nothing of these matters at the time, and I arrived at the ashram, announcing myself as an officer of the Canadian High Commission. The residents welcomed me with a great flourish and told me they were seeking enlightenment under the tutelage of their guru. I spent some time seated next to the guru who had the congregation sing for me. I recalled the refrain "…. Ram, Ram aya hei" (God, God has come).

When I mentioned that I understood the words of their devotional song, the Guru said, "The God, in this instance, is you, sir."

I thought this was too much. There are enough people who might think they are gods, but I was certainly not one of them. When I went back to Delhi and told my colleagues about my encounter, they were incredulous and thought I had temporarily lost my mind. As far as I was concerned, the ashram residents were very friendly and harmless, and they never made any demands of me in Kulu.

* * *

The NHPC, the Indian agency responsible for the execution of the Chamera Dam Project, was chaired by Mr. B.R. Oberoi. A contract to purchase Canadian equipment was held up because the official complained the price was too high and that there were no competitive bids. I argued the price was set under Canadian competition under the terms of the Loan Agreement. In addition, any delay in the purchase would impact the completion of the Dam. It was a 570 megawatt structure that would generate a lot of revenue, and each day completion was delayed, the loss in revenue would be much larger than the value of the equipment that he was quibbling about (only about $180,000). Mr. Oberoi was impervious to my logic.

I said, "This reminds me the story of Admiral Hulsey during World War II. Faced with the Japanese advance, Hulsey wanted to divert construction equipment from building a barracks to building a runway to enable the bombers to use it. The colonel in charge of the barrack building refused to release the machines, saying he had his orders. Hulsey asked him if he was prepared to take responsibility. The Colonel said he was prepared to take the responsibility for the completion of the barracks. Hulsey said, 'I mean, will you take responsibility of our defeat? The defeat would make all your barracks fall under the Japanese.'"

Mr. Oberoi understood my point, and the contract went through.

The Chamera Dam project required that many Canadian engineers and their wives live at the project site in the mountains. Although Dalhousie was one of the summer resorts favoured by the British Raj, it was no longer a thriving hill station. The engineers' wives found the place rather dreary, and there was a shortage of good food and entertainment. It was not my duty to deal with such problems, but I visited them and suggested several activities including hiking in the Himalayas, excursions to nearby historical sites, cooking clubs, bridge club, and a reading club. I also recommended some reading material: John Keay's *India Discovered*, to start with, and sent them a dozen copies from Delhi. When I visited them next, I was relieved to find they were much happier with life in Dalhousie.

In addition to Dalhousie and the Chamera site, we also frequented places closer to Delhi such as Rajasthan, Uttar Pradesh, and Haryana. Because of the many visitors who came to see us in India, there were plenty of places Hengching and I visited many times such as Agra (for the Taj Mahal and the Red Fort), the old Mughal capital at Fatehpur Sikri, and Akbar's tomb at Sikandra. In Rajasthan, we would go to Jaipur for its forts and palaces, including the royal residence of Rambagh and the

Jantar Mantar astronomical park. In Delhi, I'm sure we managed to cover almost everything of interest that was worth seeing. From the ancient period (Delhi had been the site of seven cities) to the British Raj, we knew the sites for the Coronation Durbar, Rashtrapati Bhavan (Government House), the Mutiny Monument, Tughlakabad, Humayun's tomb, the Sufi saint Nizamuddin's tomb, and city's many colorful markets and shops. India, with its history, culture and people, was endlessly fascinating to us. We traveled all over the country and the map of India that hung in my office was covered with colored marks indicating the numerous places I had visited.

* * *

My Delhi calendar was very busy. Dr. Ashis Gupta, the director of the Indo-Canadian Shastri Institution (a cross-cultural foundation), became a good friend and I met a lot of very interesting people at his many receptions including the historian Patwant Singh, economist Dharma Kumar and her husband Lavraj, critic Amita Malik, and many others. I liked Ashis - he was unassuming and suave, and he wore his erudition very lightly. His personality and his position as the director of the Shastri Institute enabled him to develop impressive contacts among India's intellectuals and artists who would often grace his receptions and dinners. His children, were friends with Nina and Tom, and they all enjoyed each other's company at the Canadian High Commission Cabana. Ashis and his wife, Swapna remained good friends, and they would later visit us in Beijing when I was posted there. We kept in touch with each other throughout my various postings after India. Ashis's love of literature would eventually lead him into publishing, and judging from the books he has given me, the publications he produces are of very high quality. When I sent him the first volume of my version of *Journey to the West*, he offered to publish it.

My other social contacts outside of work were the result of my involvement in club life. In 1987, I volunteered to be the secretary of the Thursday Club, a group of diplomats in Delhi (but no ambassadors), who met every first Thursday over lunch. My job was to find a luncheon speaker for our monthly meetings. The Canada Fund and the Thursday Club provided forums to meet many interesting people whom I would otherwise have never met, people like Ashok Khosla, Prem Shankar Jha, Kiran Bedi, Rajni Kothari, Karan Singh, and Abid Hussein.

* * *

While posted in India, I negotiated a loan agreement for the Oil and Gas Line of Credit, another major project that used funding from CIDA and EDC. EDC wanted to charge several different fees that the Indians found onerous. In my discussions with the EDC officials, I discovered they were trying to use the concessional rate of the CIDA loan to compensate for their fees. While CIDA funding approval was $225 million, EDC wanted us to start with $150 million and then gradually increase the amount to sweeten the deal. This was not the spirit under which CIDA was offering the concession, which was intended to enable development without undue financial burden on the Indian economy. The purpose of the concession was not to obtain higher revenue for EDC. I persuaded Roger Dumelie, the head of CIDA operations in India, to disclose the amount of our loan approval to the Indians, thus detaching our loan's soft terms from EDC's negotiating tactics. At the Head Office, Art Saper was not happy because he thought this was inconsistent with being a good team player for "Team Canada." He later recognized the validity of our argument and used our strategy as an example of how CIDA should maintain developmental perspective while carrying out its proper role as a Canadian agency.

Frustrated by the slow pace of progress, one of EDC's vice presidents came to Delhi insisting that "for $450 million, they better listen to us."

I told him that the sum total of donor funding amounted to less then 3% of the Indians' budget, and that India had just turned down three World Bank loans, each amounting to about $1 billion because of conditions that they found unacceptable. I told him I didn't think the Indians would be intimidated by the amount of our loan. In Indonesia, there is a saying which can be translated as "a gecko coming on like a crocodile." I was implying that we were a gecko in the eyes of the Indians, not a crocodile. He laughed at my use of the phrase, but continued to rant about Indian intransigence.

One of my favorite projects was one that utilized the counterpart fund generated by the sale of fertilizers to build bio-gas digesters. I became an avid promoter of the digesters because of their obvious, significant merits. First, the digester used what would have otherwise been discarded (animal and human waste). In addition, it helped prevent further deforestation because it decreased the amount of wood used as fuel. The digester also saved women hours of back-breaking work cutting and collecting wood (typically women's work in the rural areas). This allowed the same women to use their time in more productive, income-generating work. Finally, the digester helped reduce eye and lung infections as there was less smoke generated than from burning wood.

In Delhi, I took on the Canada Fund just as I had done in Sri Lanka. Through the Canada fund, I supported Rajiv Gandhi's constituency and got an NGO to invite the Indian Prime Minister to attend a ribbon-cutting ceremony. I also invited the Canadian High Commissioner, thus providing the unusual opportunity for a Canadian diplomat High to have the Indian leader as a captive audience for a full hour, without any agenda except to socialize and discuss whatever was of interest.

On another occasion, Joe Clark, the Secretary of State for External Affairs, was visiting India and he wanted to see the Taj Mahal in his capacity as an official, rather than as a tourist. I suggested he visit an eye clinic funded by the Canada Fund that was scheduled to open in April. Even though it was still winter, the clinic agreed to advance the opening to February when Clark was visiting. I went to ask the NGO if it would be possible and they assured me there would be "no problem." I had lived in India long enough to know that in this country "time is not money, and 'no problem' is the start of a problem." It was December and I traveled to Agra to meet with the NGO. The clinic was far from being completed, but the building itself was in good shape, and the rooms were laid out well.

I decided to visit every two weeks to ensure that progress would proceed on schedule. When I returned in January, I was relieved to find they had the operation theatre equipment and the furniture for the waiting room and recovery room. Still, only two days before Clark's visit in February, I was shocked to see that the floor of the operation theatre was still just packed dirt. Again, the NGO told me "no problem." When I returned to the clinic the next day, there was a pile of marble tiles in the room and by afternoon, the theatre had been finished with a gleaming marble floor in perfect condition. I was very impressed. The NGO pointed to a place on the wall where they were going to put a marble plaque. Even though the plaque was not ready until the morning of Clark's visit, I was no longer anxious at all. Besides, this was not the point of the visit. The minister arrived and after some introductions, he was asked to draw the curtain covering the marble plaque. The plaque said "to commemorate the visit of Hon. Joe Clarke….." They had misspelled his last name by adding an 'e.' I hadn't seen it, but the minister's staff had and a few hours later, I was asked by one of the staff members when I intended to resign. Taken aback, I asked why and after he explained about the misspelled name, I became furious.

"Don't you appreciate the fact that the NGO made a special effort to finish this place two months in advance? They didn't have to do that! I will resign after you."

Joe Clark also noticed the mistake, but he didn't think it was a big deal. In my experience, I've found it's usually the sidekicks who are the most overbearing and insufferable.

One memorable project that we helped support was an irrigation scheme in Gujarat run by an gentleman known as Bhai-Jee, an elderly devotee of Mahatma Gandhi. Hengching and I visited him in Chhotta Udaipur, Gujarat, where he showed me his fascinating project. He built tanks that were used to charge underground aquifers downstream, not the typical function to provide for surface irrigation. He covered the water with a plastic film to prevent evaporation so the water could seep underground and charge the aquifers. Standing at a high vantage point, we could see green patches of crops, even though the area was suffering from the third year in drought.

Bhai-Jee was a consummate story-teller. He told me about his presentation to promote tree-planting. He presented two men to his audience, one had a full head of hair and the other's bald head was clean-shaven. Then he poured water on their heads, and said to the audience, "See? If you have no hair on your head, it will not retain water. So the mountain needs trees to keep the rain water in its soil."

Bhai-Jee also ran "Lok Adalat," the People's Court, where he adjudicated and arbitrated disputes between parties. Remarkably, his decisions were accepted by the formal court of law. He held court in an informal setting, under the shade of a large Banyan tree.

I asked him what if a murder was the subject of a case. He told me there had been several murder cases. A man had killed his debtor who refused to repay him even though he had money to throw a party. Bhai-Jee's verdict was that the killer should work on the victim's farm to support his widow and children until the children were grown up. This was acceptable to the widow, and the murderer's sentence continued for many years. When the victim's daughter married, the murderer provided the dowry and wept at the ceremony. Bhai-Jee kept a record of all his Lok Adalat cases, which were apparently even well-known to jurists overseas. In fact, as we were taking leave of Bhai-Jee, a group of Dutch jurists had just arrived to meet with him and study the Lok Adalat.

Another interesting project was the Arpana Charity and Research Foundation. At first, when the Arpana group approached me claiming to be a religious group, I declined their request for funds because I thought they were similar to the Hare Krishna movement. Then I visited them in Madhuvan, Haryana, and I was impressed by their work. We provided a fund for the construction of a clinic. Subsequently, they asked me if they could use the fund, which was initially intended to build a two-storey building, for a three storey building instead. They had saved some money because the carpenters, masons, engineers, and architects had volunteered their time and labor. We agreed to revise the agreement and a while later, I organized an excursion to visit them with my colleagues from the High Commission's Immigration Section. I thought that the immigration officers usually saw some of the worst segments of the Indian population - those who were all too willing to lie, cheat, and circumvent the law. Consequently, their view of India and Indians was very negative. I thought a visit to people like the Arpana group ("family" as they called themselves) would be beneficial in giving the officers a better perspective on Indians that might lend some balance to their negative opinions. The visit was a success, and many of my Immigration Section colleagues stated that if more Indians were like "the family", they would happily live in India.

An unexpected result of this trip involved one of my visitors, Ann Johnston, a secretary to the High Commissioner. Ann had been trying to adopt a baby in India and was having no success. During our visit, she mentioned her plight to Mr. R. Sabharwal, Arpana's director.

Sabharwal said, "We picked up a baby girl this morning, abandoned in a ditch. Maybe it is providential that you are here. I shall see how we can help getting her adopted by you."

The adoption came through within a few months at minimum cost to Ann. Before her posting ended she was able to take the little girl back

to Canada. This was an incredible outcome. Her adoption was almost
a miracle since most took a long time, often more than a year, and
involved untold expenses and aggravation caused by the massive and
unsympathetic bureaucracy. Years later, Mr. Sabharwal came to Ottawa
and stayed with us. During his visit, he saw Ann and her daughter, the
little girl that his "family" had saved from the ditch.

One of our earliest Indian friends was the vivacious film and media
critic, Amita Malik whom we'd met at one of Ashis Gupta's receptions. We
had her over to our place many times, and she joined us for drives outside
of Delhi. Amita was married to Iqbal Malik, who was one of the founding
lights of Doordarshan (Indian national TV). It was a Hindu-Muslim love
match, and apparently a happy one until Iqbal found someone else and
divorced Amita. She took the divorce with great magnanimity, and when
Iqbal's new lover deserted him after he fell seriously ill, Amita took care of
him until his death. I deeply admired her capacity to love and her quality
of mercy, and we became good friends. Iqbal's apartment near the Qutb
Minar was vacant after his death, and it was bequeathed to Amita. She
wanted to sell the place, but I advised her not to because it was in good
condition, in a good location, and it would appreciate in value. But she
told me she did not want to keep the place that had too many painful
memories.

Amita had introduced us to Komal G.B. Singh, who struck me as
the most beautiful woman I had ever seen. In addition to her physical
beauty, she was very well-educated, sophisticated, and gentle. Amita
also helped me obtain a membership to the India International Center
(IIC), an exclusive club whose membership consists of a "Who's Who"
of India's cultural and intellectual stars. I had been unsuccessful in my
application until Amita vouched for me with the President of the IIC,
telling the board that it was making a big mistake rejecting me as I was
one diplomat whose love for India was genuine. She said that I was "such
a 'desi'" (native). She told them that if membership were to be awarded
to any foreigner, I should be a primary candidate. Within a week the IIC
notified me that I had been admitted as a member of the Center.

In turn, I would invite Amita to anything I thought might interest her,
such as the time when Jitindar Majitiya, cousin of the famous Indian
painter Amrita Shergill, came over for dinner. The story of how we met
Amrita Shergill is also an interesting one. In the summer of 1988, we had

dinner with the writer and historian, Patwant Singh just before we left for Kushinagar and Kapila Vastu near the Nepalese border. When Patwant Singh learned of our trip, he insisted we visit the Majitiyas, friends who ran a steel mill on the outskirts of Gauhati. We flew to Gauhati and took a car through the rough countryside to find Joan and Jitindar Majitiya. Just as we'd given up hope of ever finding them, we suddenly came upon the mill.

I introduced myself to a man sitting in front of the office.

"You do not know me, but our mutual friend Patwant Singh told me that I must pay you a visit if we are in your neighbourhood. So here I am, Y.C. Pan, a Canadian diplomat, and with me are my wife and Mr. and Mrs. Hanss Rackl, a German diplomat, and his wife."

Jiti welcomed us and invited us to his home. His mansion appeared like a mirage, a most incongruous vision of opulence and elegance in the middle of the ragged, impoverished looking countryside. Jiti introduced us to his Australian wife Joan, and we joined them for a wonderful, delicious dinner. He was a fascinating man who owned an airplane and had piloted the first plane to fly into Nepal. At their mansion we saw a dozen tiger skins, trophies shot by Jiti in the fifties. He invited us to stay with them, but as our luggage was at the hotel, we had to decline. He made us promise that on our return from Nepal two days later, we would stay with them.

* * *

In early 1989, the Canadian High Commissioner traveled to the far north-eastern corner of India visiting the cities of Imphal in Manipur state and Kohima in Assam, to honour the Canadian soldiers who were killed during World War II and buried in Kohima. We had some conversations about the Japanese invasion of India in 1944, and the High Commissioner invited me to join him on the trip. We laid wreaths on the Canadian graves and visited the Government Agent's residence, once the site of a Japanese sniper attack. An old cherry tree on the edge of the lawn-tennis court marks the furthest point reached by the Japanese military. When the last sniper had been shot dead by the Ghurkhas, the Japanese forces retreated. The tree has many bullets from that fight still embedded in its tough bark.

Later that same year in May, I went to a farewell party for a Korean friend of Hengching's. At the party, I was talking to an elderly gentleman named Jacob and General Batra, who mentioned that he had just returned from Imphal. We debated the Japanese decision to invade India at that time. I believed it was one of the most stupid decisions made by the Japanese military that ultimately resulted in the deaths of thousands of soldiers from disease and exposure - all for nothing. Mr. Jacob disagreed with me.

"You are wrong. I was there during the war, and the Japanese almost got us. If they had gone to Dimapur instead of Kohima, they would have taken our supplies and we would have been in deep trouble. The Japanese commander Mutaguchi was a smart man."

I told him that I'd read the Japanese High Command documents, and knew that Mutaguchi was a nut and an idiot, in addition to being ignorant, narrow-minded and vain. When asked how the long supply line could be function without air cover, and how the invasion could succeed without heavy artillery, Mutagachi replied that the Imperial Army had the benefit of divine protection.

As we argued, our host walked up to me and said, "Well, I see that you are having a lively discussion with General Jacob." I was stunned to find I had been arguing with General J.F.R. Jacob, the strategic genius of the 1971 Indo-Pakistan war, and the man who engineered a campaign for Bangladeshi independence. The brilliant General had achieved complete victory within eleven days. I sheepishly apologized for my presumptuousness, but I maintained that Mutagachi was an idiot. The General was very gracious and complimented me on my knowledge on the Imphal campaign. After that, we struck up a close association, and both of us regretted having met only a few months before I was to leave India.

* * *

In 1989, I had another opportunity to visit the northeast when the Canadian High Commissioner traveled to the Himalayan kingdom of Bhutan. It so happened that CIDA was funding an English teaching project managed by the World University Service of Canada (WUSC). I asked the WUSC project manager, Howard Solverson, to organize the visit, and we flew to Gauhati, Assam and then headed northwest driving through Bhutan to the capital, Thimphu. The Bhutanese capital is nestled in a valley of the same name almost 8,000 feet above sea-level, running along the Thimphu Chu River. The city is framed by high green mountains on either side. It is a spectacular location.

En route to Thimphu we encountered a rock-fall blocking the road near Tongsa, in central Bhutan. A work crew was still clearing the huge rocks from the road when we arrived. I thought the rock face above the road was still unstable, so I suggested that we get out of the car and walk over, with the car following us. No one wanted to get out of the car, but I jumped out of the Land Cruiser and ran the 200 meters across the rock-fall site. The car passed without incident, and every one laughed at me.

WUSC Project Manager Howard Solverson organized our trip so that we visited one or more Canadian English language teachers in his project on each day of the trip. One of the teachers named Sarah had fallen ill a few months earlier. She lived and worked in the mountains about an hour's walk from the national highway where one could catch a daily bus to Thimphu. Sarah was in too much pain to walk and I had to help arrange for an Indian Army helicopter to take her to Calcutta. As soon as she recovered (from a kidney stone), she wanted to go back to where she worked. When we visited her there, we had to leave the car and walk for an hour to her village which was very remote. She taught at the temple in the village.

When we arrived, a resident monk greeted us in the Queen's English, "Where do you chaps come from?"

We told him we were from Canada, and he said with a sigh, "Such a remote place."

I was struck by the austere living conditions that Sarah and the other Canadian teachers endured in Bhutan. They were young people in their twenties, working for little pay, and living in remote villages often without running water, indoor plumbing, newspapers, radio and TV, or even electricity. They slept in wood-frame beds stuffed with rough straw, and their rooms had no heating. Yet when their one-year contract came up for renewal, all of them extended their stay. Even after such a serious illness, Sarah still wanted to live there. I asked them why they were so insistent on staying on in such a remote and trying place. I found that almost all of them had suffered some recent personal difficulty such as divorce or a break-up, the infidelity of a spouse, betrayal by siblings or friends, losing a loved one, and even nervous breakdowns caused by financial, emotional, or physical problems. The project must have been a way to escape, or a way to find some relief from their pain, as they were completely cut off from the rest of the world. Howard acknowledged my observations, but he told me it wasn't a matter of concern because the teachers were doing a good job, and were well-liked by their communities.

On our third day in Bhutan, a Bhutanese official from their foreign ministry joined us in the town of Boomthang. He travelled with us in our Land Cruiser and on the following morning, he had a female companion join him in our car. I thought this was inappropriate, and when I asked who she was, he said she was a girlfriend. Since the High Commissioner said nothing, I said nothing. Apparently, in Bhutan the custom of "night-crawling," which was also practiced in Tibet, was still quite popular. A male visitor (the "night-crawler") would leave his shoes at the door of the girl's home, and other would-be night-crawlers would know to stay away as the girl was occupied that night.

Along the way, we visited the Tongsa Zong and met with the Dasho, or headman, who was dressed in a traditional pyjama-like costume and wore a sword. He did not have much to tell us about Tongsa. After five days of hard driving, we finally arrived in Thimphu and soon after, we met with Father McKie, a Canadian Jesuit who served as a tutor to the King's father. Father McKie had been awarded Bhutanese citizenship. We brought several cases of wines and liquor for a reception, but the hotel charged corkage fees of $10 per bottle. Scandalized by such outrageous costs, we protested loudly to no avail. We took the bottles away with us, as their was no way in hell that we'd leave them for the hotel.

On the day of our departure, the High Commissioner overheard the pilot say that the plane, a 12 passenger Dornier, was full. Further, on such a warm day, because of the altitude and the thin air, it would be safer to take off with just 10 people. As we taxied down the runway, the pilot pointed out a pile of rocks a few hundred yards in front of us and fast-approaching. The pilot had started from the very beginning of the runway to try to clear the rocks. It was a hair-raising experience, and looking out the window as we became airborne, the boulders seemed inches away and I thought I could practically reach out and touch them.

* * *

One of CIDA's projects in South India was the Idduki Hydro Power dam which accounted for 60% of Kerala's power supply at that time. I took over this project in 1986 and the first time I traveled to Trivandrum was also my first time in South India. I was captivated by the lush, green landscape in this part of the country and the lilt of the Malayalam language. I still recall the Padmanabhaswamy temple which was ornately carved with hundreds of gods and figures, yet still seemed somehow soothing to my eyes.

I stayed at the Kovalam Beach Hotel and I did not know that the beach was a dangerous place where hundreds had drowned. From the top of the rock cliffs, the waves crashing over the rocks appeared to be about a foot in height. I climbed 100 meters down to the foot of the cliff with the intention of just dipping my feet in the Indian Ocean. After I scrambled down to the shoreline, an eight-foot high wave rushed in and knocked me off my feet into the water between the rocks. Frightened and somewhat in shock, I quickly crawled out disregarding the slipper I'd lost, and climbed out of the way before the next wave arrived. When I told this to the Chairman of the Kerala State Electricity Board, he just shook his head and said I was very lucky.

In the south, I also accompanied the High Commissioner to Cochin, where I asked our host to take us to the synagogue. Our first stop turned out to be a church. I wanted to see the synagogue not a church, and it was getting late. Our host ushered us inside and showed us a brass plaque that marked the burial site of the Portuguese explorer Vasco da Gama. He had been buried here until his son arrived eight years after his death, exhumed his remains and brought them back to Portugal for reburial. The church was an interesting colonial structure that had rows of manually operated fans ("punka") hanging from the ceiling. The punkas were operated by peons outside, so that the European congregation could sit with cool air circulating throughout the church.

When we finally arrived at the synagogue, we were greeted by a gentleman who introduced himself as a Jew. His name was Jacob Cohen and he told me that the Jewish community in Cochin had 900 years of history. The first Jewish settlers traveled down the coast from Persia, and at one time there were over 3000 Jews in Cochin. But now there were only 78, mostly elderly, because the younger generation had all emigrated to Israel. As we spoke, another man joined us and Mr. Cohen introduced him as "Isaak Ashkenazy, also a Jew." Remarkably, both Sephardic and Ashkenazy Jews had come to Cochin, but I wondered how much longer the city's Jewish population would remain? The next year, I returned to Cochin and visited the synagogue where Mr. Cohen recognized me from before. When I asked him how many Jews were still living in his community, he said with a note of sadness in his voice that there were only 75.

* * *

After four years in India, I had accomplished the four things I had set out to do: 1) Travel throughout the country; 2) Meet the locals; 3) Learn the language; and 4) Study the history. Still, India left me mesmerized and smitten.

The famous economist Joan Robinson said, "India is so big, so old, so diverse, and so contradictory that, whatever you say about it, the exact opposite would be equally true."

I truly believe that you can be taken out of India, but you cannot take India out of yourself.

12

JAPAN

....

Towards the end of my posting in India the Canadian High Commissioner, Jim Harris, asked me what my plans were. I told him of my disappointment with his department when I had tried out for a posting in Tokyo. As I was now going back to Canada, I would be interested in spending a year or two at the Japan desk. Without my knowledge, Harris wrote to the Assistant Deputy Minister, Jeanne McCloskey, to recommend me for the Japan desk. While I was in Bombay organizing a visit of the National Defence College, I received a phone call at the Taj Hotel where I was staying. It was Colin Russel, director of the Japan Desk, and he offered me the position of Deputy Director of the Japan Desk. I accepted his offer, but indicated that CIDA had to be consulted. The very next day, David Spring of CIDA called to offer me a cross-posting to Bangladesh. I declined his offer because a move from India to Bangladesh would not have the freshness of going to a completely new environment, and it might also prove slightly depressing for me.

The decision to work for Foreign Affairs on the Japan Desk was an interesting and educational experience. The Trade Promotion Program was somewhat misdirected. For example, they put most of their resources into the U.S. market. This decision was based on the logic that the largest and most important market for Canada was the U.S. and therefore required the greatest support from the Canadian Government. I thought the logic was backwards because the US maintained its position as the largest Canadian market because they held a major comparative advantage for Canadian goods and services and vice versa. This condition was a fact regardless of any government support. The government should devote its resources to trade promotion and concentrate on defending the legal rights of Canadian businesses, negotiating favourable conditions for Canadian businesses in the U.S., ensuring a "level playing field", and mediating in disputes. Trade promotion resources should be devoted to markets where demand for Canadian goods and services are not well developed, especially in developing countries where CIDA programs could help promote Canadian interests.

My assignment gave me several opportunities to visit Japan on different missions, and it allowed me to observe the Canadian Embassy's operations Tokyo. Although the work of a trade commissioner was not very interesting, the position seemed worthwhile because it provided me with opportunities to experience Japanese society and culture in greater depth.

The assignment enabled me to meet some very interesting people. Okada Kaname of the Japanese Overseas Economic Cooperation Fund was one of the Japanese "experts" who came to Ottawa and gave a presentation on the workings of the OECF as part of my "Third Country Cooperation" project. The aim was to enable Canada and Japan to work together in a third country on development assistance. Okada was a Zen enthusiast who spent several hours meditating every day. He had married an American woman and when his wife was diagnosed with cancer, he agonized over it despite the serenity he'd achieved through meditation. His response to his wife's illness was very endearing to me, as it reflected his humanity. At one point, we discussed opening an orphanage after we retired. Had I not fallen ill, I would have been happy to join him in this endeavour.

I worked hard, and did well, but I was ready for another posting. Despite investigating an overseas posting in Tokyo, I started to slowly lose interest in working for the department, even if it allowed me to get the Tokyo posting. I went to see David Holdsworth, CIDA VP for Asia, and told him I was interested in a posting to China. Holdsworth recalled my presentation for the China Country Program policy and he instructed the China Desk to consider me for the directorship of field operations. In the summer of 1991, I was given the China post only two years after leaving India.

13

SECOND POSTING IN CHINA
··

When I returned to China for my second posting, it was just Hengching and myself. Our children were either in university or working, so it was only the two of us. In China, the CIDA program goal was the promotion of human rights, good governance, and democratic development. I have always believed that a democratic China under the rule of law would be a better member of the international community of nations, instead of a dictatorship where law is just the tool of a dictatorship's arbitrary will. A truly democratic China would also be less aggressive and belligerent, and less of a bully toward Taiwan. Through our efforts in China, I believe we have done a small, but significant amount of good by creating an awareness of basic rights and the expectation of accountability from the Chinese government.

When Hengching and I first arrived, we were given temporary accommodation in the Jianguomenwai Diplomatic Compound, and after six weeks we moved into the Sanlitun Compound in August. At that time, I had been called back to Ottawa for consultations, so Hengching supervised the move herself. The apartment across the hall from ours also had new occupants. Lincoln Kaye, a correspondent for the Far Eastern Economic Review, had just moved in with his wife and three children. I was familiar with his articles and over time, we developed a strong friendship. Lincoln's job put him in touch with interesting people and he shared his contacts with me, including correspondents from other papers and magazines. We embarked on many midnight excursions, tooling around Beijing, competing with each other to find the cheapest restaurants where good food could still be found for 10 yuan.

Once, we were on an outing to Tiebi Yinshan (Iron Wall -Silver Mountain), a famous scenic picnic spot, in a convoy that included other journalists. Somehow we got lost and ended up in front of a massive wall where a large group People's Armed Police guards had gathered and were nervously milling about.

We stopped our line of cars and Jurgen Kremb of Der Spiegel rolled down his window and innocently asked a guard, "Where are we? What is this place?"

One of the guards shouted nervously, "Go, go, go! You're going to be in trouble!"

Not wanting to get on the wrong side of the state police, we promptly drove away. Soon after, we stopped for directions and Lincoln's daughter, Anna said she thought we were being followed. We saw a black Mercedes stopped a few hundred yards behind us.

I gave Anna a pair of binoculars and she exclaimed; "I see them looking at us with their binoculars. When I trained mine on them, they put theirs away in a hurry."

After we arrived at Tiebi Yinshan and were laying out our rugs and preparing our picnic, the Mercedes sped past us. Jurgen told me that he'd known what the police had been guarding, but that he'd feigned ignorance. It was the notorious Qincheng Jail where political prisoners were detained. Jiang Qing (Mme. Mao Zedong) had hanged herself while in custody at Qincheng. Jurgen knew the guards would never tell him what the place was, but he wanted to see their reaction.

In late January of 1991, Lincoln and his family joined Hengching and me on our vacation touring around Fujian Province. We went to Zhangzhou, where my ancestors, Hengching's, and Lincoln's wife Meilang's came from. We were pleasantly surprised to find another connection in the street-food that was not only tasty, but very similar to what we ate in Taiwan. Unfortunately, Hengching's ancestral home had been demolished in preparation for a new department store - all that was left was a big hole in the ground. Later, on the eastern coast in Jiangxi province outside of the city of Fuzhou, we found some old doughnut-shaped buildings that had served as family-fortresses centuries ago when the Japanese pirates scoured the waters and the shore for loot. An old blind woman we met there told us that one of these structures once belonged to a Pan family and that she had a cousin who went to work in Taiwan some 60 years ago.

On the drive to Quanzhou, Hengching saw a beautiful bird fly across the road in front of our car.

She pointed it out exclaiming, "Look at that beautiful bird!"

The Chinese driver said, "Yeah, it's beautiful, but it doesn't taste very good."

In Quanzhou we found what appeared to be a pet shop. Anna fell in love with a puppy, and begged her mother to take it home. Meilang said it would be hard to take it on the plane.

The shop owner cheerfully informed us, "No problem - you can eat it here!"

In the town of Fuzhou, amidst noisy firecrackers and smoke from the New Year's celebrations, Lincoln and I saw a portrait of Mao in one of the shops along the street. There he was right next to the Bodhisattvas and the Heavenly Emperors. The shop owner proceeded to tell us that Chairman Mao was now a god who protects people from accidents and floods.

"Did you know that when students smeared the Mao portraits at Tiananmen Square, the sky suddenly darkened and sand storm began? And if you have Mao in your car, you will be spared from accidents and injuries."

I suggested to Lincoln that he write a piece on the deification of Mao. China has always had a history of worshipping living persons, and I noted that one of these living gods appears roughly every 1000 years. Before Mao, it was Matsu 1000 years ago, and 2000 years ago it was Guanyu, then Laotse, and finally Jiang Taigong 4000 years ago.

But none of the gods ever intervened to save us from the catastrophic Chinese bureaucracy. My very first encounter with this frightening institution involved the arrival of my personal car. I was told to leave one or two cartons of American cigarettes in the trunk for the customs inspectors. One of my colleagues whose car was also arriving at the same time was outraged and refused to put anything in his trunk. I understood the Chinese character better than he did. If you challenge their authority, they become twice as nasty and will take great pleasure in their victory over you when you finally submit to their demands. This was not an issue to which I wanted to devote a lot of moral and political energy, so I provided the cartons of cigarettes and received my car two days later. It all turned out very differently for my colleague who was told that his car's brakes needed adjusting. When he next inquired about his vehicle, he was told that the headlights were not centered. A while later the customs inspectors notified him that his tires were not balanced. After suffering through a series of such tactical manoeuvres and with considerable disgust, he finally provided the requisite cartons and got his car two days later.

The maintenance at our apartment was handled by the state's Diplomatic Services Bureau (DSB) workers who refused to lift a finger after three-thirty in the afternoon. One day we had a problem with our plumbing and Hengching called them. It was two-thirty, so someone came. At three-thirty he was preparing to leave even though the work was not finished.

Hengching asked him "What happened to the spirit of Lei Feng?"

He scoffed and said, "Lei Feng is forgotten."

The next day when he showed up again, Hengching offered him beer and a pack of Marlborough cigarettes to finish the job and he stayed after three-thirty. We had established our reputation as people who would provide extra rewards.

After that, whenever Hengching called the DSB workers' depot, they would say, "It's the Canadian Embassy apartment? Someone will be there right away!"

* * *

Immediately after my arrival in China, I noticed there were many interesting things happening in various development agencies such as the World Bank, the United Nations Development Program, the Ford Foundation, the Konrad Adenauer Foundation, and the Republican International Institute to name a few. However, there was no mechanism that allowed for any coordination between the numerous individual projects. I took the initiative and wrote a circular to the heads of these organizations proposing to organize a forum for kindred spirits, the "Development- wallahs" as I called them. I suggested that we get together and network over lunch the first Thursday of every month. I asked my friend Tony Azarias, Manager of the Zhaolong Hotel, for a special lunch rate and a private room for about fifty people. For the first session I invited William Hinton, author of a definitive report on land reform after the revolution and a friend of Mao Zedong and Zhou Enlai, to give the first keynote speech. It was a great success and the "Development-wallah lunch" became an institution with regular participation from the World Bank, the UNDP, and other major foundations and NGOs. It was a totally informal body without name, charter, membership, head, or even a secretariat. Before leaving China, I handed it over to another Canadian, Brian Bedard, but my successor, Hausing Tse, decided that this sort of thing should be operated by the embassy. Hausing Tse ran the lunches for about three months, but then I learned that without my network and personal involvement the whole thing eventually fizzled out.

A little bit of encouragement went a long way in China. Whenever I used an embassy vehicle for personal purposes, I was supposed to rent it with a DSB driver. I would give the driver 100 yuan for soft drinks and snacks, and after my excursion was over, the driver received any left-over beer and food from my reception or meeting. Consequently, whenever I wanted to rent a vehicle, the drivers would vie for the assignment. Every Christmas I gave the drivers and maintenance crew a few bottles of whiskey and gin, along with a few hundred yuan "for snacks." The result was that I had no problem asking for maintenance for our Development Section. These were not considered bribes. As I was their superior, they viewed my generosity as a show of respect in the traditional Chinese manner.

My first exposure to the pernicious nature of the Chinese Communist system was my experience with the DSB. Three competent Canadian officers under my charge were assisted by two local officers assigned by the DSB. The Diplomatic Services Bureau controlled all personnel and a property used by the Diplomatic Corp, including our personal servants and our living quarters, and the bureau was hated by all. In those days, it was impossible to hire local employees except through the DSB. Although I found Mr. Hong Binwen and Mr. Li Qingdong to be reasonably pleasant and adequate English-speakers, the DSB was run mostly by bureaucrats who behaved no differently from thieves and crooks. They considered the poor workers under their charge as objects for exploitation, and would bully them into surrendering the year-end bonus they received from us. These payments were gifts expressing our good will and weren't part of the DSB contract. In the "Workers' Paradise" that was communist China, a government agency was exploiting the workers worse than any capitalist or Mafioso. They demanded that the DSB workers surrender the presents of bikes, radios, TVs and the like. All of our Christmas gifts, intended to compensate for the cash bonus that they lost to their greedy managers, were also taken away. We took serious offense at this situation, and decided to subvert the DSB whenever we could. As Christmas drew near, I summoned Mr. Hong and Mr. Li individually to my office, gave them cash gifts and told them it was between the two of us and that DSB had nothing to do with it.

Meanness and corruption were not confined to the DSB. The selection of candidates for a fellowship program that was managed by the embassy to finance Canadian studies for Chinese scholars was entrusted to China's Ministry of Foreign Affairs ("Waijiaobu"). For the past few years before my arrival, the program had become very unpopular at the participating Canadian universities which hosted the Chinese scholars. Many of these so-called "scholars" never even attended their designated universities, which had made room for them in their offices by moving out Canadian students. It turned out that the scholars were actually just friends and relatives of Waijiaobu officials. Most of them could not speak English and had nothing to show in the way of any scholarship related to Canada. Sometimes, they lived in cramped conditions, four to a room, in Chinatown, earning money by washing dishes.

The Embassy forwarded universities' complaints to the Ministry and requested a more careful selection process be implemented. As expected, the Ministry insisted that those selected were the best they could find. Richard Burton, the embassy's program director asked me what to do about this issue. I suggested that we advertise the availability of fellowships in academic magazines, clearly outlining the benefits and requirements such as the ability to speak English or French, a proposed topic of study, and any publications on Canadian topics. Next, we should test the applicants. Richard decided to take my advice and we wrote to Waijiaobu about each step we intended to take. The Ministry ignored every letter we sent them, without even acknowledging their receipt. We went ahead with the advertisements and received a very enthusiastic response from many genuine scholars. Next, we selected the most qualified candidates for interviews, and presented our picks to Waijiaobu requesting that chosen individuals be issued passports.

The Chinese officials were considerably annoyed by our initiative, as they would certainly lose face to the friends and relatives they had promised a perk-filled, lucrative trip to Canada. Not long after the selection was made, Richard and I were meeting with the Ambassador when there was a commotion in the Immigration office. The "scholars" who had been selected by Waijiaobu, had come from all parts of China to protest their exclusion. Although Richard spoke Mandarin, he deliberately addressed them in English. None of them understood a word he said. As Richard's questions were translated - "Do you speak English? We have advertised in several magazines asking for application. Why did you not apply?" and "Why are you here?" The group became furious.

"You are abusing our human rights," they shouted.

Of course, Waijiaobu had refused to issue passports to our selected candidates. We suggested to the head office that the fellowship program be cancelled unless the selection process was more disciplined and transparent. They agreed, and Richard notified Waijiaobu that we were prepared to cancel the program.

The Ministry began panic and they appealed to the Ministry of Foreign Economic Relations and Trade (MFERT), our main contact in China. I was called by MFERT, and told that we should not let Waijiaobu lose too much face. After I told them the whole sordid story, passports were issued and we continued with the program but on our terms.

* * *

In addition to our major projects, I managed a million dollar budget for the Canada Fund which was used to support projects in places that our other funds and programs did not cover. Hengching and I had a lot of fun on the Canada Fund visits that included trips to Tibet, South Gansu, Qinghai, and Zhejiang. We saw many innovative projects such as the "village water main" project in Lhasa, which eliminated gastro-intestinal diseases that had once afflicted 80% of the village's 2,000 inhabitants and cost only $5,000. There was the "ground hardening" project in Gansu that collected rainwater in a cistern that was then locked to prevent theft. Prior to the introduction of the cistern, villagers would climb down the hill and walk for miles to the river to collect water. Of course, we will always remember the "pig fattening" project in the ancient Silk Route town of Wuwei, where for a few thousand dollars, plastic covers were provided to farmers' pigsties to keep their pigs warm and help fatten them up over the winter. It was very satisfying to see how a few thousand dollars could make such a significant and sustainable difference to so many people's lives.

Our Silk Road trip took us from Dunhuang, down the Gansu corridor to Lanzhou via Jiuquan, Zhangye, and Wuwei. Apart from the projects we saw, this excursion was also a memorable journey because of the beautiful religious art that we were able to see. The arid climate had almost perfectly preserved the ancient caves at Dunhuang and their serene, yet colourful Buddhist paintings, and I remember the monumental reclining Buddha at Wuwei – so much larger than the one I saw in Kushinagar, Nepal.

In December of 1991, Hengching joined me on my trip to Tibet. Bruce Jutsi, the embassy's officer, wanted to report on the human rights situation in Tibet, but he could not get permission to travel there from the Chinese government. Bruce used the inspection of the CIDA Canada Fund Program as a pretext to go to Tibet.

With our wives joining us, we flew to Chengdu where we were met and feted by the office of the Chengdu Management Training Project. Before our flight to Lhasa the next day, the officers took us to the grave of the famous Chinese hero, Kongming and the home of the great Tang poet Du Fu. Kongming was an important character from the *Romance of the Three Kingdoms*, a story I'd read as a young man in Taiwan and one that I also read to my children. Du Fu lived in the eighth century, and is considered to be one of the greatest Chinese poets. He is often paired with Li Bai, whose poems were more spontaneous. Western comparisons liken Li Bai to the sonatas of Mozart, whereas Du Fu's work is more like Beethoven's symphonies. Like Mozart and Beethoven, the two poets also knew each other. I felt very inspired after visiting these two historical sites in Chengdu.

Before we left Beijing for Lhasa, we were cautioned that there was only about 65% oxygen content in Tibetan air because of the high altitude. We were advised to take oxygen pumps with us, not to walk too fast, and to never run. I didn't feel the need to use the pumps on our trip; however, Hengching had a harder time. She could not breathe lying down, so she slept sitting up, and was sleep-deprived throughout our entire stay. To add to her suffering, she found the smell of yak butter intolerable, and she could not drink the yak-butter tea that was such a ubiquitous part of Tibetan social life.

The Potala Palace, once the seat of the Dalai Lama, rises out of a massive stone hilltop in Lhasa like a white cliff topped with red roofs and turrets. The place has an otherworldly quality about it, yet this did not alter the bad behaviour of the Chinese soldiers at the site. Some of them were visitors, but the others were guarding the palace (from whom I wondered). On our visit to the Potala, I was offended, but not surprised by their cultural insensitivity. Here, in this beautiful and historic place, the soldiers spit out their chewing gum, talked and shouted loudly, and made a general nuisance of themselves.

The state officers of the Tibet "Autonomous Region" who were our hosts, both of them Tibetans, were wary and did not trust me because they thought I was Chinese. I told them I was Taiwanese not Chinese, and that I sympathized with their cause. Then I showed them my photo with the Dalai Lama at his home in Dharamsala taken in 1989. One after another, the Tibetan officers touched the photo to their foreheads as a sign of respect and devotion to their spiritual leader. After that moment, they seemed to trust me completely.

The effects of the Chinese policy to stock Tibet with ethnic Han people was visible everywhere. The streets of Lhasa and other towns took on the appearance of the average, dreary Chinese city, with drab cement buildings, wide and barren streets, and Chinese banners extolling the virtues of the Communist Party. We met a few foreigners at the Holiday Inn's "Tin Tin Café." One was a school teacher from California whose son's letters arrived with Chinese notes inside. She could not believe how clumsy and stupid the Chinese state could be, that they were not even concerned about disclosing their censorship of private correspondence. I suggested that maybe the Chinese wanted her to know she was being censored. She should be careful of what she wrote. I took a few letters from another hotel guest, a Canadian teacher, to send out via diplomatic pouch to her family. I will never forget one Tibetan I met in Canada many years later during the Dalai Lama's visit. She said that she wept when she saw the Tibetan spiritual leader. And she went on to describe how the Chinese bosses in her homeland were dishonest, highhanded, corrupt, and mean. I told her that I was not surprised. Chinese officials are like that in Beijing and even in Taiwan, why should they behave any differently in Lhasa?

* * *

In China, corruption was everywhere. When I traveled to the poorer regions in the countryside, I often saw the officials whose projects we were funding, driving around in a shiny new Mercedes Benz, while I, the donor-representative was traveling in a Toyota. In the provinces, host officials would organize dinner and luncheon parties of three or four tables seating 30 - 40 guests on the host's side, compared to one or two diners who were with me. My visit gave them all a pretext to throw a feast. We established a Project Support Unit to look after the logistics of incoming missions and the embassy officials' needs with regard to travel, meetings, and accommodations. This was actually MFERT's job, but we wanted to relieve this burden so they could concentrate on more substantive program issues. Nevertheless, we needed permission to allow our funding to be used for such purposes. MFERT refused to sign the permission for a long time. I tried to resolve the issue and thought I'd succeeded, only to be told that the MFERT director wanted us to provide a car for MFERT before he would grant permission.

Once, a team of Canadian physicians visited Ningxia, one of the most impoverished provinces in north-western China. They were appalled at the poor state of healthcare in this forlorn region. After they returned to Canada they appealed to several major hospitals to donate medical equipment that was still in good working order, but was obsolete because of new, technological advances or surpluses. They gathered together a freight container full of X-ray machines, EKG and dialysis machines, and other important, life-saving equipment. The physicians would pay all the expenses to ship the container to Ningxia, and they asked me to obtain a duty-free permit for import. Chinese Customs imposed a duty of about U.S. $100,000. I explained that the used equipment had no commercial re-sale value and was intended for use in Ningxia. I argued that Ningxia desperately needed the medical equipment and not only were they unable to pay the duty, imposing it was inconsistent with the Chinese Government's policy of helping the poorer regions. The Customs official was impervious. Clearly, they were waiting for a bribe. I could not comply, so I asked one of my acquaintances, a senior official in the Communist Party, if he could help. He agreed to do something, and I told Ningxia they might get the equipment after all. I was subsequently informed by the same senior official that while he was successful in removing the duty, he still had to decide where the equipment should go. It would not be Ningxia, as he knew "where the need is greatest." I couldn't believe it. I had expected help, not hijacking. In the end, I told the official and Chinese customs that the equipment would be shipped to India where tax exemption was not a problem.

In the vast and most distant western region of China, near Tibet and central Asia, was the city of Urumqi, once a fabled stop along the Silk Route in what is now Xinjiang province. The first time I visited Xinjiang was with a CIDA-funded Anti-Desertification Project in collaboration with the Qinghua University. The Taklamakan Desert, the largest in China, was advancing quickly and competition for land and its resources was becoming a problem between local Uygurs and the Han migrants from the east. This was the result of the Chinese Government's policy of transplanting large numbers of Han migrants as part of their "Populating the Border" policy. Disputes were brewing between the Han migrants, mostly over the allocation of water. I watched the agonized deliberation among mostly Han officials, over the profligate use of water by those living upstream who were causing droughts downstream. Urumqi was taking on the dreary look of the average Chinese city, with the same, monotony of ugly buildings and barren streets lined with Chinese shops. The city was expanding because of oil exploration, and most of the beneficiaries were Han. I accepted an invitation to dinner from a local Uyghur family, and I sensed their resentment against the Han Chinese. Still, they were reticent and careful in my presence. I had to assure them that I was not Han Chinese. They were still not very comfortable around me. This troubled me, so I explained that I was a Canadian originally from Taiwan, and that I understood their plight. I made sure to speak when there were no Han Chinese around us, and this relieved their anxiety. The Uyghur family talked about rising up against the Chinese, but I advised them not to, as they were no match against the well- armed, ruthless Chinese communists. Any uprising would only result in Uyghur bloodshed and their sacrifice would achieve nothing.

They were angry and frustrated and asked me what I thought they should do instead. I told them their only salvation lay in the democratization China. They should support countries like Canada in the hopes that they would succeed in bringing democracy and the rule of law to China. Only under the rule of law would the abuse end, and the Uyghur people gain a measure of respect for their human rights.

* * *

In China, we could still catch a glimpse of the ancient, imperial world beyond the monolithic shadows of the state communist apparatus. Princess Aixinjueluo Xianqi, also known as Mme. Jin Moyu, was the last living princess of the Qing Dynasty, the last imperial era when China was under Manchu rule. Born in a palace, she was raised as a princess even though the Qing Dynasty had collapsed in 1912, two years before Mme. Jin Moyu's birth in 1914. She lived in Manchuria which later became Manchukuo, a Japanese puppet state, and she attended the Japanese Peers' College. At the end of World War II, Mme. Jin Moyu returned to Beijing, and after the revolution, she was imprisoned under a trumped up charge. She had spent the best years of her youth in prison. Fourteen years after incarceration, Mme. Jin Moyu was told the initial accusation against her was found to be baseless. However, in an incredible example of further injustice and arrogance, the Communists claimed her attitude during her incarceration had been "incorrect," and sent her to a labour camp for seven years. After her release, she wrote a memoir in Japanese. When I read it I was amazed that there was no bitterness over her years of suffering in the Chinese camps, and no resentment toward those who conspired to imprison her. Far more important than her imperial lineage, Mme. Jin Moyu's noble spirit enabled her to transcend the tragic circumstances of her life under the communists.

When I first arrived in Beijing, I asked my assistant to find Mme. Jin Moyu's contact information.

I called her and introduced myself, "Madam, you do not know me, but I am an admirer of yours from reading your memoir. I wonder if it would be possible to meet you and so that I may pay my respects."

She casually said, "Are you free at 11 this morning? Come to the Beijing Hotel. I will be there at 10:30 to say goodbye to Countess Saga, the widow of the last Emperor's brother."

That is how our friendship with Mme. Jin Moyu began. As a princess, it was not surprising that she enjoyed a great deal of attention, especially in Japan. Every year, she was invited to Japan, where she stayed at the most luxurious hotels and mansions, many of which were owned by her Japanese classmates. In China, she lived in a shabby, one-bedroom apartment in the eastern outskirts of Beijing, and yet she seemed as comfortable in her friends' mansions as she was in her humble apartment. She would return from Japan with many trunks filled with presents from her Japanese friends, and in a gesture of royal nonchalance, she would give many of them away. Knowing my fondness for Japanese sweets, she brought back the most expensive Yokan, a delicious red bean paste dessert from Toraya, Japan. Once, she even knit a sweater for Nina.

Although she was capable of great consideration and generosity, she often treated those around her like personal servants. After knowing her for a year, I came to believe that her attitude of not regarding people as equals must have been ingrained in her from a very young age when she was raised as a princess. It may have explained why she did not resent those responsible for her imprisonment, as she would not condescend to make them objects of her resentment. I began to suspect that her generosity and kindness toward me might be that of a master to a servant. And little by little, my attitude toward her changed. While I still admired her nobility of spirit, I no longer wanted to be seen as a supplicant. Once, when she was recounting how strict the old Manchu protocols were and the importance of social ranking, I interjected and said, "Aren't we all glad that we're not living under that kind of rigid and unfair system?"

After a pause, she coldly replied, "Indeed."

After we left China I tried to phone her a few times without success. She no longer lived at the old address that I knew, and our communication faded. When I first met Mme. Jin Moyu, she was 77 years old, yet she had the energy to start a Japanese language school with funds donated from her Japanese friends and the Japanese embassy. The last I heard of her was that she'd moved the school to Langfang, just outside of Beijing, on the way to Tianjin.

* * *

During the White Terror of the Kuomintang in Taiwan, people spoke of Chen Bingqi in hushed tones whenever his name was mentioned. He was my uncle's cousin and had been broadcasting from China throughout the 1950s and 60s, inciting the people of Taiwan to rise up and overthrow the Kuomintang government. In those days, Taiwan was a police state and tuning in to an enemy broadcast from China could land one in jail or worse. Still, his name was spoken with some admiration and a great deal of curiosity. I say admiration, because he was so critical of the hated Kuomintang, and curiosity because China had remained such a mysterious taboo all those years. I never met him while I was in Taiwan, and I'd only heard vague rumors about him.

His name came up again years later, in 1973 when I met his cousin, Tommy Chen (also known as Xiao Chen or "Young Chen"). When Xiao Chen learned that I had visited China in 1972, he said it was unfortunate we'd not met earlier because he could've introduced me to his cousin Chen Bingqi (who was known as Lao Chen or "Old Chen"). Finally, in 1983, I met Lao Chen for the first time. I asked him how he ended up in Beijing. He told that when he was in his teens, he rebelled against Japanese colonialism that had made the Taiwanese into second-rate citizens in their own homeland. As an adolescent, he often got into fistfights with the Japanese, but quickly learned that this was not a solution to the problem of the imperial Japanese in Taiwan. After agonizing for a long time, he decided to join the Chinese Kuomintang's fight against Japan. He'd managed to raise some money for a trip to China, but before he could leave Taiwan he was caught, tortured, and ultimately released for being a minor.

At the close of World War II, with the collapse of Japanese colonialism and the Kuomintang's ascendancy in Taiwan, Lao Chen welcomed the people of the "Motherland" and he joined the Kuomintang Youth Corp. But he quickly found the Chinese to be corrupt, arrogant and incompetent, far worse than the Japanese. Again he agonized, and his young mind began to absorb forbidden thoughts. In those days books of "subversive thoughts" previously confiscated by the Japanese censors had re-emerged and were available at many roadside shops. Inspired by Kobayashi Takiji, Kawakami Hajime and other Japanese left-wing writers, Lao Chen decided that Taiwan's salvation lay in socialism. In the immediate aftermath of the 228 Incident in 1947, he organized his fellow students against the Kuomintang. Wanted by the police, Lao Chen was on the run for over a year in Taiwan, hiding at his cousin's house, working in a gold mine, and sometimes sleeping out in the open. Finally, with the help of one of his friends who turned out to have been a Communist, he escaped to China via Hong Kong.

Once in China, the Chinese Communist Party (CCP) leadership told him to go back to Taiwan because the Taiwanese Communist Party had been decimated. With considerable courage and determination, Old Chen returned to Taiwan to work as an underground recruiter for the

Communist Party for about a year. This man who had fought against colonial injustice as a teenager impressed me and, although I did not share his ideology, I admired his idealism, passion, and courage.

Then in 1987, I learned about another side of Lao Chen. It all began with a biography of Hsia Suat-hong written by one of my acquaintances, Chen Fang Ming. Like Old Chen, Hsia had also fled Taiwan to avoid execution by the Kuomintang after the 228 Incident. He went to China where, in the 1960's and 1970's, Hsia was persecuted by the CCP for advocating communist rule for Taiwan that was separate from China. In this very well documented biography, Old Chen was described as one of the CCP's agents who tormented Hsia. I was scandalized. Lao Chen seemed to have lost his earlier idealism and passion for Taiwan, and had sold out to the Communist Government of China.

When we arrived in Beijing in June 1991, I did not seek out Lao Chen. But as fate would have it, one day A-hok, the manager of the Zhaolong Hotel across from my apartment, phoned to inform me that there was someone at the hotel who wanted to meet me. He would not reveal the person's identity over the phone. Curiosity got the better of me and I went over to the hotel with Hengching where we found Lao Chen and his wife Dr. Duan Aifang. A-hok had already told him that I was in Beijing on a posting as a Canadian diplomat, so I could not escape contact with Lao Chen. I decided to find out how he would react to the biography of Hsia Huat-hong and I lent him my copy. I warned him that there were several unflattering references to him, but that I was interested to hear his response.

Lao Chen read the book and told me it was valuable for being so well researched, and that it contained many sources that were not easily available. Overall, it was a commendable scholarly effort, but the references to him were inaccurate. He proceeded to explain that he did not persecute Hsia, and his wife, Dr. Duan, corroborated his story. I was impressed by his willingness to acknowledge the value of a good book, even though it contained an unfavorable reference to him.

Our association with Chens resumed and we became very fond of his wife, Xiao Duan, or "Little Duan" (as she is fondly called by her husband and friends). Together, we visited many points of interest in and around Beijing, and we covered almost everything any visitor (or resident, for that matter) could hope to visit, and then some – old temples, tombs, monasteries, palaces, hot-springs, handicraft factories, pearl dealers, antique shops, and even museums that were not open to public.

In April 1996, I was in Taiwan when Lao Chen came to visit. I wanted him to meet with Chen Fangming to discuss the Hsia biography in the interest of historical accuracy and to restore his reputation. He was curiously reluctant. Prior to leaving, I asked Lincoln Kaye to ensure that the meeting took place. After my departure, Lincoln wrote, "Our friend, Lao Chen (also known as Chen Dapao, or "Chen the Big Cannon" for his daring and outspokenness), was nervous as a cat, looking over his shoulders for signs of secret agents – from China? Taiwan?" I thought it was comical that Lao Chen would feel so self-important as to think he'd merit Taiwanese or CCP surveillance. The meeting did not produce anything, Chen Dapao stood his ground, and Lao Chen did not offer any credible challenge.

Over time, I gradually found Lao Chen's wholesale acceptance of Chinese Communist propaganda too much to swallow. He believed the U.S. bombing of the Chinese Embassy in Belgrade was deliberate. He believed the Chinese system under the CCP was the best in the world and that it brought unprecedented prosperity for everyone. He believed the Chinese media was unbiased and that it cited many reports from overseas. Although he accepted that widespread poverty remained a real problem throughout the country, he was convinced that the regime was doing enough to mitigate its effects. He even denied that there were millions of victims of corruption, expropriations, and serious pollution in China.

After the 2008 Olympic Games in Beijing, Lao Chen told me that spectacle demonstrated the superiority of the Chinese system compared to the rest of the world. He said that the Bush family had come to China to seek money. He dismissed as "Western anti-Chinese propaganda" the proposition that the Chinese Olympic performance was only possible under a dictatorship that could spend money without accountability, and that the training of athletes had resulted in thousands of youths who did not make the finals and were left without education or skills to find jobs. Lao Chen would not accept the notion that human rights abuses existed, or that highhanded censorship had resulted in many foreign reporters being beaten up.

As for the many victims who were forcibly moved from their homes to make room for the Olympics, he blithely dismissed their grievances saying, "They should be willing to make the sacrifice for an important national priority."

With his faith in the system and the CCP, I found it futile to argue with Lao Chen and I gradually distanced myself from the man.

14

TAIWAN

In 1992, while I was still in Beijing, Eiji called me from Taipei to ask if I had any plans to travel to Japan. He had learned that Prof. Peng Mingmin would like to see me. Prof. Peng was my hero. He was a graduate of McGill and a star professor at Taida. In 1964, after he wrote a manifesto for Taiwanese self-determination (*A Manifesto to Save Taiwan*), he was arrested and sentenced by a military court to eight years imprisonment. There was a global effort protesting his sentence by overseas Taiwanese, including many of his former students, who appealed to U.S., European, and Canadian governments and media for his release. I worked with Morris Cohen, Dean of the McGill University Law School, to mobilize support among Prof. Peng's classmates, and in the process I worked with John Fenston who I helped translate Prof. Peng's manifesto into English. I also made an appearance on TV to denounce the Kuomintang and to make an appeal for international pressure that might secure Prof. Peng's release. This effort produced a positive result and Prof. Peng's sentence was commuted to house arrest for life. In 1970, he escaped to Sweden and then became a lecturer at some of the best American universities. He finally returned to Taiwan in 1992 after he was granted amnesty by Taiwanese authorities almost 23 years after his escape.

Although I had no immediate plans to travel to Tokyo, I told Eiji that I would make myself available if Prof. Peng wanted to see me. Hengching and I traveled to Tokyo and booked into the Hotel New Otani. I met with the Professor and after some initial pleasantries, I told how I admired his courage and asked what I could do for him as a Canadian diplomat based in Beijing. He thanked me, but did not say anything more.

I tried harder and said, "You have now been back in Taiwan for some time. You must have a lot of plans. I wonder if there is anything I can do to help."

He said nothing so I continued, "Sir, you know that you command a great deal of respect in Taiwan. We all look up to you as our moral leader whose political wisdom we respect. I know that you must be under great pressure to make yourself available as a candidate for presidency in the 1996 election. But I would like to suggest that you resist the temptation to run. As you know I spent four years in India. In India, Nehru commands a lot of respect as one of the founders of independent India and its first prime minister. But even greater respect is given to Gandhi, who had never occupied any official position but acted as the moral authority above politics. I would very much like to see you in the role of Gandhi rather than Nehru, because Taiwan badly needs an iconic figure. I hope you will take this into consideration."

He did not respond to my suggestion, and after some more trivial conversation, he left. Hengching looked at me and we both wondered aloud "what was that about?"

After our strange meeting, I saw Eiji and asked him if he knew why Prof. Peng had wanted to see me. He was as puzzled as I was, and I teased him for making me come to Tokyo at great expense for nothing. I suppose Eiji should have asked Prof. Peng why he'd requested a meeting and what we needed to discuss, but we assumed that it must be a substantive matter that Prof. Peng did not wish to disclose. We took his request on faith, because we held him in such high regard.

It turned out that Prof. Peng did not take my advice and he ran for presidency in the 1996 election, only to lose. Despite my earlier objections to his candidacy, I returned to Taiwan from Canada to support him in the election. The day after the polls were counted, he invited Eiji and me to a dinner. He was in a despondent mood, which was understandable because he received only 21% of the votes.

I told him, "You should not feel too bad about the election results. When you look at the results from the point of view of Taiwan as a whole, we had a great victory. Mr. Lee Tenghui got 54% of the vote, so together with Prof. Peng's 21% share, the Pro-Taiwan vote came to 75%. Now we can show China that the Taiwanese have stood up to their rule."

As I was leaving the Beijing post in 1994, I went through Tokyo to meet with Prof. Mineo Nakajima, a staunch supporter of Taiwanese independence. I told Prof. Nakajima that the Taiwanese people were grateful for his support, but I deplored the inadequacy of Taiwanese diplomacy in Japan. Too often, relations between the two countries were handled by incompetent diplomats who were often hostile to the idea of an independent Taiwan. For example, as Eiji helped Vice Prime Minister Xu Lide make contacts with ranking Japanese bureaucrats and politicians when Xu attended the Asian Olympics, the Taiwanese Representative Office tried to sabotage his effort. After I'd returned to Canada, Eiji phoned and told me that Prof. Nakajima had spoken to President Lee Tenghui and suggested there were two Taiwanese he should meet - Y.C. Pan and R.T. Peng. Unfortunately, it would be difficult for me to meet President Lee as I was residing in Canada.

I used to tease Eiji that he got to know Lee Tenghui because of my meeting with Prof. Nakajima. I did not meet Mr. Lee until Eiji and I worked on a project with Israeli experts on a national survival strategy for Taiwan. During that project Eiji finally introduced me to President Lee. I had long thought that Taiwan could benefit from Israel's experience in developing a national survival strategy. Eiji and I began a collaborative effort and I wrote a proposal for the project. Our efforts were successful and Eiji received funding to consult with Israeli experts on military strategy, U.S. relations, military-civilian social relations, military-industrial strategy, and sea defense. I asked Prof. Martin Rudner of Ottawa's Carleton University to provide the names of experts in these fields and I recruited some of them to visit Taiwan. I also traveled to Israel with Eiji and several senior members of Taiwan's defense establishment to consult with their Israeli counterparts.

* * *

There was another occasion in November 1999 when I worked with Eiji to benefit Taiwan. I proposed a concept paper for the establishment of a NGO dedicated to the international promotion of Taiwan. At that time, the Taiwanese Ministry of Foreign Affairs could not accomplish certain things because of Taiwan's lack of diplomatic relations with most major countries. My brother-in-law, Robert Wenlong Chen, assisted me with the paper, which was very well received. Working on this project required that I leave my job as the head of the Canadian Aid Program in Poland and travel to Taiwan to help Eiji present the project concept to President Lee. The President was impressed and agreed to provide initial funding, but at the last moment he suggested that we wait until after his term expired in 2000. He believed that Lien Chan, the Kuomintang presidential candidate, would take over and that Lee would remain as chairman of the Kuomintang in charge of vast amounts of funding. I objected to this plan because there was no guarantee that Lien Chan would win the election, and even if he did, there was no guarantee he would do as Lee asked. And if Lien should lose, how would Lee be able to mobilize government funding? I urged Eiji to persuade Lee to provide the funds immediately, but he was not successful. Ultimately, Lien lost the election and Lee not only ceased to be president, he also lost his chairmanship of the Kuomintang. The project was never funded.

In September of that year, there was a major earthquake in Central Taiwan that caused many deaths and thousands of people were rendered homeless. Eiji managed to obtain 1000 prefabricated houses from Japan at no cost. They had been used to accommodate victims of the earthquake in Kobe, and the Japanese had stored them in a warehouse after the city's reconstruction. Eiji was able to mobilize a shipping company that provided ocean transport free of charge, and he also secured trucking companies to move the materials from the port to the construction sites free of charge.

When I arrived for the presentation of the concept paper, Eiji had been invited by President Lee to attend the inauguration of the housing scheme using the Japanese prefabs. Since I was arriving from Poland, Eiji declined the President's invitation. President Lee was so anxious to have Eiji attend that he told him to bring me along in the presidential jet to Central Taiwan for the ceremony. It was the first and probably last time I flew in that jet and shared the presidential cabin with Mme. Lee, while the minister of defense and other officials sat in the passenger cabin. It was a taste of real VIP treatment. I tried to think of conversational subjects as I chatted with the first lady. The media had reported that she was an aficionado of opera. So I proceeded to recount my story of being sick in Italy, and how I had to communicate with the attending physician (who did not speak English) in phrases from various Italian operas. Mme. Lee had no idea what I was talking about.

* * *

As my posting in Beijing was drawing to an end, Pierre David, the director-general of the Policy Service and Program Operations Division of the Partnership Branch (PSPO) contacted me about another position. The PSPO Division performs a staff role, providing advice and recommendations on policy and operational matters of the Partnership Branch, which handles private businesses, NGOs, universities, institutions like AUCC (Association of Universities and Colleges of Canada), labour unions, and churches, etc. As I did not have any particular plan or job obligations at that time, I accepted his offer.

One of my first tasks was to formulate a policy regarding CIDA contributions in support of Canadian businesses that wanted to invest in developing countries. The policy issue had been in development for over a year, and I arrived to find eight draft proposals that had been presented and rejected. I quickly read the memos, and decided that they were totally inadequate. Together with the consultant, Bill Guest, and the Policy Branch adviser, Sadruddin Rahman, I boiled the issues down to three points which I presented in a three-page memo to the minister. I recommended that 1) We keep consistent records on the performance of CIDA funding recipients, including information available for analysis, periodic evaluation, and reference; 2) We stop requiring recipients to repay contributions when they do not proceed to invest because the cost of collecting repayments was greater than the funds recovered - Instead, I recommended a stricter application screening process before approval to ensure high performance; and 3) We raise the minimum volume requirement of annual business per applicant from $100,000 to $1,000,000.

The four years I spent with the PSPO were not very eventful, as it was primarily a desk job. My only real excitement came from my extracurricular activities, such as the development of the national survival strategy for Taiwan with Eiji. Thankfully, that collaboration got me out of the office and took me to Israel twice. I did get to Paris several times while I was with the PSPO because I was also the CIDA representative to OECD. My visits to Paris deepened my dislike of the city, which struck me as phoney, pretentious, self-centered, and unsympathetic. I never developed such antipathy toward any other city. In all of my travels around the world, I always found something I loved in every city – except for Paris!

15

POLAND

Ever since I visited Russia for three weeks with Hengching 1996, I had wanted a posting in Moscow. Our trip there was at the invitation of Donna Rainbow, my former secretary in Beijing whose husband Maurice had been posted to Moscow. We stayed at the Rainbows' apartment in the capital for a week and visited the usual tourist sites like the Kremlin and Red Square. We also went with the Rainbows to Yasnaya Poliyana to pay our respects to Tolstoy and to Sergeev Posad where I stumbled upon the grave of Boris Godunov. After Moscow, we spent a week in St. Petersburg and saw the requisite places of interest there including the Hermitage, the Peter and Paul Fort, the Nevsky Cathedral and Cemetery, and we even lunched at the Literatura Café where Pushkin had his last supper. After St. Petersburg, we returned to Moscow for another week of historic sightseeing and our extensive use of the Moscow subway system gave us a taste of modern Russia. On one occasion, we stopped at every station to enjoy the ornate and beautiful designs while trying not to think of the slave labour and the workers that might have perished during its construction. As a result of our trip, I was deeply impressed by Russia and the Russians. In 1997, when the posting cycle for the following year came around, I put my name in for Moscow.

One day after lunch, for absolutely no reason that I can think of today, I took the elevator instead of following my usual routine of climbing the stairs to my office on the 11th floor. Alex Volkoff, head of the CIDA Poland Program, was in the elevator and after we'd exchanged greetings, we both got out at the 11th floor (Alex's office was on the 12th floor). Out of the blue, Alex asked me if I'd be interested in a posting to Warsaw. Her question took me off-guard and I replied that I'd rather go to Moscow.

She said, "That's next door, and you have great music in Poland."

Alex urged me to put my name in for Warsaw, which I did, however, I also wrote down Moscow as my first choice. Alex must have pulled a few strings, because I ended up being nominated for Warsaw. She later told me that she was agonizing over recruitment for the Warsaw position until she ran into me on the elevator.

I was expected in Warsaw by the New Year, but I agreed to visit Poland for a month in early 1998 to meet with Ottfried (Otch) von Finkenstein, the incumbent in my post, and to familiarize myself with the CIDA program. My visit would coincide with the Supervisory Board meeting of the Canada-Poland Entrepreneurs' Fund (CPEF) in Gdansk. At the meeting, I realized the Polish side did not understand how CIDA funding worked and this was a problem as I would be a future member of the Board. After communism collapsed in Poland, the CPEF was established with a Canadian fund earmarked as part of Canada's contribution to the Polish currency stabilization scheme. Even though the fund was never utilized (because the Polish zloty stabilized), the Poles thought the fund belonged to them and they repeatedly asked when the full amount ($27 million) would be remitted.

As an observer in these proceedings, I sensed that Otch, being a Foreign Service officer, had not explained how CIDA's funds work. I took the initiative and explained that the $27 million did indeed belong to Poland. It was the basis for the negotiation to set up CPEF. But CIDA funding was not cash in bank and therefore it could not simply be remitted. In fact there was no cash, only CIDA's authority to draw up to $27 million from the Canadian Government's Budget to pay for authorized disbursements. Money was withdrawn only when funds were disbursed under specific projects. I suggested that the best way to get the full amount was to make the CPEF work. Loans against the fund would be disbursed and when the total amounted to $27 million, Poland would have received the full amount. My explanation seemed to have quieted down the Polish side.

After the CPEF's initial stumbles, CIDA ultimately succeeded in disbursing the $27 million during the four years that I was posted in Poland. The bulk of the hard work was done by the CPEF staff, led by its new and very capable president, David McRae. Later, as a member of the Supervisory Board for CPEF, I would visit the town of Szczecin (Stettin) many times where the CPEF offices were located. It is a very German-looking town with a church where Catherine the Great of Russia had been baptized.

* * *

My formal posting in Poland started in April 1998. On my way to Warsaw, I attended a CIDA field representatives' meeting at Lake Balaton, Hungary, where I met colleagues in postings ranging from Russia, the Balkans, and Turkey to far-away Kazakhstan. At night, we were entertained by dancers who performed the "czardas," a traditional Hungarian dance, with great vigour and passion. I remember there was with a lot of jumping and boot-slapping, which reminded me of the nomadic Magyar blood that still ran in their veins.

Initially, I moved into Otch's former residence in Wilanow, south of Warsaw near the Palace Wilanowa. Later, in June, I moved to Kossaka 4 in Zoliborz, the northern part of Warsaw. Our residence was next to the church where Jerzy Popielszko, the "Solidarity Priest" had his parish. There were three things that stood out for me in Poland. First, Polish streets are filled with memorials to those who fought and died for the nation's independence. Many of these "pomniks" had fresh flowers, evidence that people still remembered and cared enough about those who had sacrificed their lives for Poland. Second, I was struck by the pro-Western sentiment in Poland. The people were still grateful to the Americans for their liberation and they were connected by family ties to large Polish populations in the U.S., the U.K., and Canada. Third, even though I have seen many beautiful women in many countries, the Slavic women were the most beautiful in the world. Per capita, there seemed to be more pretty women in Poland, and I joked that I used to fall in love with at least three women everyday when I took the buses and trams from the embassy back home.

* * *

I met the renowned political scientist Zbigniew Pelczynski after I rejected his funding request for not meeting our guidelines. I was intrigued by Zbigniew, an Oxford professor in Poland trying to train a generation of new leaders. He was born in Warsaw and as a youth under German occupation, he had joined the underground resistance. Even though he was captured by the Nazis, somehow he escaped execution. During his captivity he learned German and English, and after the war he went to Edinburgh to study, eventually ending up at Oxford where he became Professor of political philosophy and an authority on Hegel. In the 1980's, after the Solidarity Movement had been temporarily crushed, he organized a fellowship to bring Polish students to Oxford, and in the 1990's, he organized leadership training for young Poles. He wanted to put the political theory he was teaching into practice and he felt that Poland lacked an entire generation of political, economic, and civic leaders. The reason for this lack of leadership was that under the communist dictatorship of the Eastern Bloc, people learned to be either subservient or rebellious, but not democratic and law-abiding.

Zbigniew's program was very successful in training more than 4000 young people, including many leaders in political, commercial, and social fields. Some of the trainees eventually became ministers in the new, democratic Polish government. I found Zbigniew's concept of leadership training to be quite remarkable, and I envied the fact that as a Pole, he shared such a strong sense of national identity with his countrymen. It was this national identity that served to bind the population with such solid cohesion. Unfortunately, such a scheme would not be so easy in Taiwan where there was no consensus on national identity.

I admired many Poles like Zbigniew, who cared deeply about the health and direction of their nation. Halina Niec, a law professor at the University of Krakow, ran a human rights centre in Krakow. I visited her several times and was impressed by her dedication and brilliance. In 2001 I organized a class reunion of my Taida Economics Class of 1957, 40 of my classmates visited Krakow and they listened to Halina who spoke, at my invitation, about the development of Polish national identity. She gave a brilliant talk at the restaurant Hawelka, and I have never heard such a cogent and amusing presentation. Prior to my departure from Poland, she came to my farewell dinner which proved to be our last meeting. Sadly, she passed away a year later when I was in Kiev.

Monika Platek was another law professor who taught at the University of Warsaw and ran a NGO for women's rights. We met after CIDA funded one of her workshops that explained the rights of women in marriage. She introduced me to her colleagues in Russia and Ukraine, and consulted with me in developing her workshops. Monika was a kindred spirit who I introduced to Zbigniew Pelczynski and together, we developed a training program for women leaders.

I started a small group of music lovers in Warsaw, and Monika was a core member of our informal club. We would gather once a month or so to listen to recorded music and I was impressed by Monika's knowledge of Russian folksongs. She introduced me to some very good music including Bulent Okzawa, Dzana Vichevskaya, and Ivan Revrov. She also introduced Mercedes Sosa whose haunting voice conveyed the forlorn passions of the Argentine working class. These evening get-togethers are one of my fondest memories of my time in Warsaw. We would play CDs of our favourite music, have dinner, and play some more. The format was simple in that each participant would play one or two pieces, no more than four minutes each, explain what the piece was, why it was chosen, and what to listen for. This resulted in educational and enjoyable evenings with Monika, Krzystof Pavlowski, Mark and Sasha Bence, and a few others as the main members, with the Canadian ambassador Don MacLennan joining us later.

* * *

The city of Poznan is famous for its early resistance to Communist rule in 1956. In June of that year, workers went on strike and their protests grew, culminating in attacks upon the headquarters of the Communist Party and its secret police. In the rioting that followed, dozens of protesters were killed. But Poznan was also a beautiful medieval city where the first Polish cathedral had been built. I visited a military cemetery near Poznan where dozens of Canadian soldiers, killed during World War II, were buried. These were airmen and many of them participated in the "Great Escape," a mass escape of American POWs from a German camp that was later dramatized in the film starring Steve McQueen and Lee Marvin. For each of my four years in Poland, I participated in Remembrance Day ceremonies honouring the Canadian soldiers killed who lost their lives in World War II. These were always moving events, and it was heartening to see that the Poles remembered the sacrifice and were still grateful to the Canadians for their help. Every year, the Polish authorities sent two soldiers to stand guard at the memorial site where they presented their guns and laid a wreath with the inscription "With the gratitude of the Polish nation."

Interestingly, Poznan had been under Prussian control for almost 130 years when it was known as Posen. In the 18th and 19th centuries many Polish cities and towns were considered parts of Prussia, Pomerania, and Silesia - all areas under German control. Hengching and I traveled extensively throughout the country. We visited the Mazovian Lake district where the late Pope John-Paul II used to spend his summer retreat in the monastery of Wigle. We spent a night at Jan Strumilo's, a poet-painter and breeder of beautiful Arabian horses that Hengching adored. The region included Wolfsschantz near the town of Ketrzyn/Gierloz where Hitler built his headquarters to conduct his Eastern Campaign and where Claus von Stauffenberg attempted and failed to assassinate him. I saw the bunkers, many of which had been destroyed as the Germans retreated in the face of the advancing Red Army. It was creepy to see such places and hard to imagine the mentality of those huddling in these sepulchral structures from which they ran their evil empire.

One of my favourite and most frequently visited sites was Chopin's birthplace at Zalazowa Wola - we took all of our guests who were visiting from other countries to such places. The city of Gdansk was not far from the largest Teutonic Knight's castle in Malbork. It was striking that Gdansk looked remarkably similar to German cities such as Frankfurt, Hamburg, and even Munich. It was hard for me to imagine that this was the birth place of Solidarnosc, the non-communist trade union formed in the Lenin Shipyards that grew into a broad anti-soviet movement and led to near-free elections in 1989. By the time I'd arrived, Lech Walesa, the former charismatic labour union leader and ex-President, seemed more like a blundering bumpkin who received only about 3% of votes in the most recent elections.

Hengching and I visited Krakow on many occasions to see several CIDA projects including the human rights training program headed by Prof. Helena Niec. My assistant, Dorota Blicharz, thought Krakow was the most beautiful city in Poland and she dismissed Warsaw. I disagreed with her. Warsaw is a lovely city, with many beautiful places spots and parks, but it is also beautiful because it embodies of the spirit of Poland and its many stories of resistance, uprising, sacrifice, and hardship. Admittedly, Krakow is very interesting as the northernmost aesthetic expression of the Italian Renaissance, and the spirit of that epoch is still visible in many of its old buildings. Thankfully, the city was spared heavy destruction from aerial bombing raids during World War II, and there are many interesting buildings still intact. In the Royal Palace there is a small brass plaque with an inscription that reads "The people of Poland are grateful to Canada, which kept the Royal Treasures of Poland during World War II and returned them to us after the War." The city also has other points of interest nearby. One of them is Auschwitz-Birkenau, the site of a Nazi concentration camp, where I also took my guests visiting from abroad. Some of them said they did not want to visit this place of death and cruelty, but after they went, they were glad they did. Also near Krakow is the Wieliczka salt mine where one could descend 190 metres (out of a total depth of some 500 metres), and see the many underground facades and cavities created by the excavation of rock salt. There is even a huge cathedral carved out of salt where some couples have their wedding ceremonies.

* * *

In Poland, I took credit for a number of important changes. First, I managed to have John Spikerman removed as president because he was unfit in that role. He refused to get to know his own staff, refused to have any contact with the clients (borrowers), and he refused to socialize with his Polish counterparts including the president of the Pomorski Bank, the Polish executing agency. I introduced CPEF to the Small Business Incubators project, another CIDA project aimed at fostering micro-businesses in need of loans. And finally, I used the Canada Fund to support several projects in the Szczecin area to enhance the image of the Fund. But looking back on the four years I spent in Poland, what I remember most about the place are the people I met – both Poles and expatriates.

One of these expats was Shining Sung a Taiwanese woman born in Tainan. She was a childhood friend of Huang Meihsing who I had met in Taiwan. In 1999, Meihsing was a senior adviser to Taiwan's Ministry of Foreign Affairs and she asked me to meet her friend Shining when I returned to Warsaw. Shining was returning from Moscow where she was helping to set up a restaurant at the Bolshoi Theatre in Moscow offering menus of the House of Romanov, the last imperial Russian dynasty. She was spending a couple of days in Poland, and we met over for a long and leisurely lunch. Shining's Japanese was excellent, an unusual trait for people of her generation in Taiwan. No doubt she polished her language skills attending the prestigious Aoyama College in Japan. Shining was a sort of cultural entrepreneur, arranging cultural events such as concerts, exhibitions, shows, and festivals. She knew many Polish scholars and artists, and introduced me to scholars such as Karol Mysliwiec, a noted Egyptologist, and Jerzy Axer, professor of Classics at Warsaw University, among others.

After Shining returned to New York, she wrote me a glowing email saying the two hours she spent with me was an inspiring experience. I did not even recollect what we discussed, perhaps something about Taiwan or Poland, but nonetheless we began a correspondence. It is curiously wonderful that such a long-lasting friendship could develop from an encounter of only two hours over lunch.

In 2000, when I was going to Taiwan, Shining suggested that I meet her uncle, one of the richest men in Taiwan, but also a well known lover of great art and music. Apparently, he had opened a large museum that was stocked with art works which Shining had helped purchase on his behalf. I went to Tainan to meet her uncle, but he was not available. Still, I had a good look at the museum which was quite impressive, albeit slightly disorganized.

Then in 2001, before Hengching and I traveled to Taiwan, I asked Shining if she was going to be there at the same time. She was, and she invited us to a concert she'd organized, featuring the Polish-American pianist Ruth Slecynska who, despite her advanced age (80), played three major concertos in one evening – Liszt, Tchaikovsky, and Chopin. This was the second time Shining and I met.

Over the next few years, we would find ways to meet up at various events around the world. We saw an exhibit of Russian paintings at the Guggenheim Museum and then went out for a sumptuous lunch. In 2007-2008, Hengching and I went to Beijing for my fourth stem-cell treatment. Shining was in the Chinese capital for only three days, but she made time to come and visit me at the hospital. I was really touched by her kindness and consideration.

During my posting in Warsaw, I was looking for information on NGOs that were active in Belarus. When I visited the Institute for Democracy in Eastern Europe (IDEE), they invited Pawel Kazanecki and Mark Bence to meet with me as they were the most familiar with NGO activities in Belarus. Mark had been running civil society development projects for George Soros in Belarus. His efforts were so successful that he was kicked out of the country by President Lukashehnko's police. Mark would prove to be very generous with his time and resources when I asked him to evaluate project proposals coming from Belarus. Even though I was not living in Belarus and had no representative there, I was able to fill a program budget of $150,000 per year with his assistance. I felt guilty about asking Mark for so much help without being able to pay him, but he said he would be happy to help so long as it was beneficial to Belarus. Mark was a friend and eventually he also became a core participant in the music club I'd organized in Warsaw.

After removing John Spikerman from the CPEF, we asked David McRae (who was then VP of CPEF), to assume the position of CPEF president. Since his takeover, David vigorously promoted the loan program for small and medium enterprises, frequently visiting the branches of the Pomorski Bank that served as the disbursement conduit administering the Canadian loans. Under David's leadership the CPEF became a going concern and was finally regarded as an active institute that belonged to post-communist Polish society.

Like me, David was a history buff and he lent me many biographies of historical personages like Talleyrand, Catherine the Great, and Rasputin. Whenever I visited Szczecin, David and I would have dinner and visit one interesting place or another. We went to Bolno Slinovo, formerly a major German army base with huge facilities to service tanks, and a house that was the residence of Hans Guderian, the innovative German military theorist and general of the Third Reich. The facility had been inherited by the Soviets after the war, and it subsequently served as a major advance base near the East German border. There were large rows of tank garages, with rusty tank repair facilities rotting away. There was a cemetery nearby that contained a numerous children's graves and it was truly heart-rending to see so many toys left from 1991 on the unkempt graves.

16

BELARUS

In the summer of 1999, for reasons that were unclear to me, the Canadian Government switched the diplomatic accreditation for Belarus from Moscow to Warsaw. Consequently, CIDA's responsibility for the Belarus program fell on my shoulders. I asked my colleague Eric Yendall in Moscow about our program in Belarus, its content, budget, and policy.

Eric's reply was simply, "Zero. We have no program there. As long as Lukashenko is president, we have no interest."

On further reflection, I felt that having "no interest" was the wrong response. Lukashenko was not the whole story. Belarus would soon sit on the eastern border of NATO, and there must be people working for democracy and human rights that were worth supporting. To test my theory, I went to Minsk with the Ambassador who was going there to present his credentials, and I asked to meet the UNDP, World Bank, USAID, and OSCE. I discovered a number of interesting things. These organizations directed many activities in Belarus and both multilateral and bilateral donors (such as the U.S., U.K., Sweden, and the Netherlands) were supporting many projects. Further, there was already Canadian funding for the UNDP to clean up the Dnieper River and as Belarus had been seriously affected by Chernobyl, a Canadian NGO, "Children of Chernobyl," was helping people afflicted by the disaster. I also discovered that there were numerous Belarusian NGOs, many of which were working with Polish NGOs.

Upon returning to Warsaw, I wrote a memo to Peter Daniel proposing that we start a small Canada Fund program in Belarus, with a budget of about $100,000 to start. Peter agreed with my suggestion and instructed Michel Lumelin, head of the Poland program, to allocate $25,000 for me to start something for Belarus. I was a bit dismayed as $25,000 was not even enough money to buy a nice car! Nevertheless, I put the fund to use, working with IDEE, a Polish NGO focusing on Belarus. With the help of Mark Bence, I managed to identify a project for grassroots democracy training using theatre and games, and a project for a conference of Belarusian NGOs to develop a consensus approach coordinating their strategies and activities. When the projects were completed, I went back to Peter and asked for more money. This time, he provided $50,000 for Belarus. The following year, a presidential election year, I wanted to support Lukashenko's opposition so I asked for extra money. In addition to the $75,000 I got for the first year, I was given another $75,000. Consequently, we had many good projects supporting the media, grassroots mobilization, awareness-raising, and election watch.

I visited Belarus a total of four times. The route proceeded from Warsaw to Brest-Litovsk, then to Minsk from where I would branch out to various parts of the country. On these quick, short tours, I managed to cover quite a bit of the country, including Glebokaya, birthplace of the painter Marc Chagall, and the aircraft designer Ilyushin. Crossing of the Polish/Belarusian border was a major event. At the checkpoint, the line-up of people in transit could extend many kilometres. Ordinary people often had to spend many hours, sometimes even days, to wait for their turn. This traffic fostered a substantial service industry near the border crossing. Villagers near the border would approach travelers and offer to wait in line in their place for a fee. In addition, the villagers would open their houses to the travelers for the night. When the traveler's turn came, the villager would call home on their cell phones, and the traveler would hurry back to the checkpoint in their car or truck.

Fortunately, because I had a diplomatic visa, my vehicle was exempt from this long line of people and my crossing took only about 30 minutes. When I went to Belarus for the last time, in 2002, I offered to take Prof. Zbigniew Pelczynski with me, as he wanted to visit some NGOs and explore possibilities for launching a leadership training program in Minsk. Traveling with me saved Zbigniew many hours of an aggravating wait.

On another occasion, IDEE asked me to transport $150,000 in cash for two Belarusian NGOs. As IDEE had helped us when we wanted to give grants to our own projects in Belarus by paying cash on our behalf, I agreed. I knew I would not be searched, but I worried more about theft or robbery than an official search. I kept the cash in my backpack, and I finally parted with it only when the recipients showed up. One of the grants was to be given to Wierzha, an NGO in Brest. I had to formulate a plan that was worthy of any plot involving international intrigue, and I asked my assistant, Kasia Kardas, to stuff the cash into a large handbag she'd brought for the transfer. Kasia then went to the washroom and hand the bag to Inna Kolei, the head of Wierza.

The annual budget of $150,000 was maintained for three years until my departure in 2002. Each time I visited Belarus (at least once a year) I met a lot of fine people including Aleksandr Salaiko, Galina Drevezova, Boris Zvzskau and his wife Galina, Inna Kulei, Aleksandr Milinkievich, and Viktor Shelkievich the poet/songwriter from Grodno. The Belarusians are very friendly, warm hearted, hospitable, and generous to their friends. Before I left Warsaw for Kiev, I hesitated to inform my Belarusian friends of my farewell party at the Embassy because I knew it would be hard for them to come all the way from Minsk, Brest, and Grodno. The dreaded border crossing alone could eat up several days. However, not wanting to feel guilty about leaving them out, I waited a week before the event to invite them. Incredibly, they all made it and Viktor Shelkievich even brought his guitar and sang "Shalonaya," the song with which he greeted me when we first met in Grodno.

17

UKRAINE

....

I was 67 years old in 2002, my posting in Warsaw was ending and I was looking forward to retirement. But then events followed unexpectedly and I accepted a posting in Kiev, Ukraine. It all began a year earlier in July, 2001 when Peter Daniel, VP for CIDA Eastern Europe, attended the graduation ceremony for the MBA class of the Warsaw School of Economics. It was the final class funded by CIDA. The day of Peter's departure, I decided to take him around the city and show him some of the interesting sites before he left. I dismissed the Embassy car, and we drove around the city in my car, before I dropped him at the airport. Standing in line to check-in, Peter mentioned my upcoming final year in Warsaw. What would I do after my posting ended? I told him I was ready to retire.

Then, I added somewhat whimsically, "Unless you want to use my talent elsewhere – in which case, make me an offer I cannot refuse."

He mentioned a consultancy in the Balkans, but I was only interested in a posting where the embassy took care of my needs. I told him that what I really wanted was a posting in Moscow.

Little did I know that I would be moving further east into what was formerly Soviet territory, but it wouldn't be Moscow. After I made a few inquiries in the autumn of 2001, Peter finally called me in early November and offered me the posting in Kiev, Ukraine. I still preferred Moscow, but Peter persuaded me that the most important program in Eastern Europe was in Ukraine

"We are a big fish in a smaller pond, while in Moscow we are a small fish in a much bigger pond."

In any event, the Moscow posting just wasn't a possibility as there were other candidates in queue for that posting before me. Hengching and Nadia were concerned about healthcare in Kiev and the radioactive fallout from the 1987 Chernobyl nuclear accident. After inquiring into these issues we were all satisfied that we'd be safe in Kiev; so I accepted the posting.

As I'd done for the Warsaw position, I offered to visit my future posting in Kiev early, in order to familiarize myself with CIDA's program in Ukraine. I met the local staff and worked closely with Valerie Sirois who was the acting head of the section. It was heartening to see their competence, dedication, and their spirit of solidarity. I heard that the ambassador, Andrew Robinson, was difficult to get along with and that he had little regard for CIDA. Initially, I approached him gingerly, but I soon found that he was not at all unreasonable and that he exhibited good political sense.

Before leaving for Ukraine, I asked some of the Taiwanese merchants in Warsaw who had business contacts in Poland and Ukraine if they knew any Taiwanese in Kiev. They told to contact Mark and Caroline Shen, a Taiwanese couple working as missionaries for a Taiwanese-based protestant church. In the summer 2002, I visited Kiev for three weeks and I met Mark and Caroline for the first time. Their church did not give them a salary or insurance, just $600 a month to cover "expenses." Such a small amount was barely enough to cover rent and food for their family of four. Yet they seemed genuinely happy and content, perhaps because their sole purpose was to convert Ukrainians to their version of Christianity. Despite the long history of the Eastern Orthodox Church in Ukraine, the Shens were succeeding in making many converts among the local population.

Hengching and I were impressed by their selflessness and genuine interest in the welfare of others, including non-believers like us. However, I found their version of faith a little hard to take. It seemed too naïve, and it anthropomorphized God which contradicted my own understanding of the divine. I could not identify with their practice of asking God for specific favours. They believed that their prayers were answered when the desired results were obtained. I was more used to believing in submission to God without any quid pro quo involving prayers. For example, they did not have enough money to pay for their son's tuition, so they prayed very hard. A few days later, their head office in Taiwan told them about a donation from a member of their congregation that was just enough for the tuition. Naturally, they rejoiced and thanked God. I was surprised that they did not thank the donor for his generosity. When my posting had come to an end and we were preparing to leave Kiev, we gave them a large tin of soy sauce and one of sesame oil. Once again, they thanked

God, as they were running out of these two items and then they thanked us, as agents of their God of course.

Their dedication and open house attracted a large crowd of Chinese students who were in Kiev. At the time, there were over 10,000 Chinese in Ukraine studying everything from Russian, to space science, to music. Many of them had converted to the Shens' Protestant faith, perhaps because having lost their belief in communism, they were spiritually adrift and open to new ideas. Gentle, honest, and friendly, these Chinese were very different from the people we had encountered in China. It may have been the result of conversion, or they may have been like that before (and that was why they converted). Two of these converts, Shi Jianya and Wu Jianming came to see me when we were in Beijing for my third and fourth stem-cell treatments.

We genuinely liked the Shens and their flock and we always felt very cosy and warm in their company. We envied them for their sense of community and for having a faith that was strong enough to console and guide them. And even though we could not bring ourselves to adopt their faith, they never tired of trying to save our souls.

During that first visit to Ukraine in 2002 I also participated in election monitoring with Marvin Wodinsky (who I knew from the Japan Desk, when he was the deputy director for India). But the highlight of my first experience in the former Soviet republic was a trip to Chernobyl, the site of the worst nuclear accident ever. The Chernobyl disaster occurred on April 26, 1986 when a nuclear reactor suffered a meltdown and released a plume of radioactive fallout into the atmosphere, reaching northern and Western Europe. Approximately 350,000 people had to be resettled, and the radioactivity in the area caused many long-term environmental and health problems including extremely high rates of Down 's syndrome, chromosomal aberrations, and numerous cancers.

Chernobyl lies north of Kiev very near the Belarus border, and the shortest route was north to Chernikhiv, and west across Belarus before re-entering the Ukraine at Chernobyl. I had a multiple-entry diplomatic visa for Belarus, but only a single entry visa for the Ukraine (which I'd used to enter the country). What would I do if the border control near Chernobyl refused to let me re-enter into Ukraine? It turned out that we re-entered Ukraine without even noticing that we'd crossed the border. We had come through at a point without any border control – probably a legacy of the old Soviet Union, when member states of the USSR did not require visas of other members' states.

As we walked towards the main building at the Chernobyl plant, I took a picture of a huge bronze head of Lenin only to be told that it was not allowed. After a presentation about the station, the disaster, and the donors helping to handle the site, we proceeded to a small museum near the actual explosion site. The exhibit showing the effects of the meltdown was nightmarish: the explosion, the contaminated workers and equipment, and the sight of thousands of vehicles abandoned as if in a huge cemetery. The nearby workers' village was now a huge ghost town, with rows and rows of apartments now abandoned for 15 years and covered by weeds and grass. The slogan "Lenin's thought will prevail!" was still barely visible on a wall. Before leaving, we went through a machine that checked whether we had been contaminated by radioactive dust. It was a great relief to finally return to Kiev. I had never scrubbed myself down so thoroughly.

Back in the Ukrainian capital, I went to the Pechersk Lavra, bastion of Ukrainian Orthodox Church (also known as the "Kiev Monastery of Caves"). Built in 1039, it was almost as old as Kiev's St. Sophia, and it was also architecturally similar with its bell-towers, cathedrals, and shining gilt onion domes. What makes Pechersk Lavra so special is, of course, its caves which are actually catacombs that form a maze of underground tunnels extending for 15 kilometres. Curious, I had no idea what to expect so I purchased a candle and entered the catacombs. This system of tunnels is actually a massive crypt for holy men who were entombed there over the centuries in coffins that lined niches along the walls. I quickly realized that the tunnel was not lit and that I was walking alone with a candle in a tunnel that was pitch-black, without any sense of direction. I didn't know where I was going and I began to panic. If my candle should go out, would I be stranded among the mummified saints? It took me a while to recover my senses, and I made it back to the land of the living without further incident.

Before returning to Warsaw, I visited the Ukrainian Academy of Public Administration which had received CIDA funding for training civil servants. Bohdan Krawchenko, the rector of the UAPA, was a graduate of McGill and Oxford universities and was well known for his efforts in this field. That first visit, we discussed CIDA funded projects and their goals and objectives. Not long after I came to Kiev to begin my posting, Bohdan complained to me about high blood pressure, and I told him that I recently began involuntarily biting my tongue and cheeks and that I was having difficulty speaking clearly. Bohdan immediately called his friend, Dr. Ludmila Verbova and insisted that I see her at the hospital. After my examination, she told me her preliminary diagnosis was that I had a progressive neurodegenerative disease called "amyotrophic lateral sclerosis," better known as "ALS," or "Lou Gehrig's Disease" after the famous New York Yankees baseball player who was diagnosed with it in 1939. At the time, I had no idea what ALS meant and did not give it much thought as the symptoms were not serious and not visibly progressing. Besides, Dr. Verbova said the diagnosis was preliminary.

Later, my friend Eiji noticed a change in my speech and word pronunciation over the phone, and he started to worry about me. At the time, I was going to visit Taiwan, so Eiji asked one of his best friends, Dr. Huang Kunyan, to find the best neurologist in the country for me. Dr. Huang recommended C.W. Lai, who was also one of my cousins. C.W. subsequently called my sister (who knew nothing of my condition) and told her he had been asked to help a Taiwanese-Canadian diplomat who he suspected was me. In Taiwan, C.W. ran some tests that confirmed the initial diagnosis of ALS. After I returned to Kiev, Bohdan was constantly worrying about my illness and he would regularly order me to visit the doctors at the clinic. Olga Brizhan, the secretary of our division, introduced me to an excellent doctor, Maria Spiridonova, who was aware of all the newest treatments and drugs for ALS. In 2004, just after I left the Ukraine, Bohdan was asked by the Aga Khan Foundation to start a university in Bishkek. Even though he virtually disappeared from Kiev, he continued to write me from Bishkek.

* * *

After a few weeks of orientation, Hengching and I settled into Kiev and moved into Marvin's former apartment on Mykyrska Botanichna (Mekbot). It was a spacious second storey flat with three bedrooms, three bathrooms, and two studies. I got to know the embassy staff, many of whom I'd met on my first visit to Kiev. Volodymyr Seniuk, the senior local officer in the Embassy's Development Section, was the first one to work with me. As a "certified" Chernobyl worker (with certain privileges that he never used), Volodymyr had taken me to Chernobyl during my earlier visit. He was so knowledgeable about Ukraine's history and culture, that I developed a habit of asking him to plan all my trips to visit projects, combining sites of historic interest en route. Along with Natalia Zavarzina, another local senior officer, they were a dependable pair that made the section function smoothly. Everywhere I went, I was impressed by how well Volodiya and Natalia were received and how well they knew the projects' details.

I never treated them as subordinates, but always as colleagues and friends. One reason for this was, apart from their competence, they were both very likeable and a lot of fun. In early 2003, on a visit to Poltava I noticed a statue of a general at the entrance of our hotel. As a joke, I asked Natalia to pose with the statue and pretend as if she were posing with her lover, the general. This became an inside joke, and wherever there was a male statue, Natalia would pose beside it as the figure's lover for a photograph.

Towards the end of my posting, we went to Kharkiv where we encountered a former Soviet office complex built so that each office building was of a distinct and different height. When I was told that the heights corresponded to the tune of the Communist anthem, the "Internationale", I began to hum it and Volodiya sang the opening line that begins with, "Vstavai!" (meaning "Rise!" or "Awaken!"). I thought he sang "Davai" (meaning "Give! or "Let's do it!") and I commented how it was in character for Communists to sing "Davai."

Natalia corrected me, "No, it's not Davai - it's Vstavai."

Volodiya added a risqué punch-line saying, "You have to Vstavai, before you can say Davai!" Meaning you have to rise, or get it up, before you can do it.

* * *

One reason I found the Ukraine program so interesting was because it was mostly driven by Ukrainian Canadians. As a result of their interest and engagement in the projects, Ukrainian Canadians also donated their own funds to match CIDA funding. One of these Ukrainian Canadians was Orest Subtelny. Before my posting had begun, the Ukraine Desk sent me a copy of a definitive history of Ukraine written by Orest Subtelny, a Ukrainian professor at York University. It was written before Ukraine became independent and it was required reading for university and college students in Ukraine. The book sold millions of copies, but its author did not collect a penny. When I met him he said it didn't matter, he thought it was part of his service to Mother Ukraine.

Orest's book opened my eyes to some of the darker chapters of Eastern European history. For example, he wrote of the many atrocities perpetrated by the Polish Szlachtas upon their Ukrainian tenant farmers He offered a revisionist view of Bogdan Khmelnitzky, vilified by Poles as the monster who slaughtered Poles. In Orest's view, Khmelnitzky was a reluctant rebel whose fiancée and son had been abducted and killed by a Szlachta. After Khmelnitzkiy repeatedly went to the Polish court seeking justice without success, he rose up against the Poles and their system. In Orest's eyes, not only was Khmelnitzky not a bloodthirsty killer, he mercifully spared Lviv after the siege.

Orest came to Kiev as the director of a CIDA project providing training and consultation to the Ministry of Foreign Affairs on "Asymmetric Diplomacy," a characterization of the relationship between Ukraine and Russia. Asymmetric diplomacy was especially pertinent to Ukraine's dealings with Russia on the Sea of Azov. Whereas Russia insisted on the "brotherly sharing" of the entire sea, international law held that Ukraine was entitled to more than 2/3 of the area. But "brotherly sharing" prevailed as Ukraine was dealing with a much more powerful Russia. The Ukrainians benefited from Canada's experience in its own asymmetric negotiations with the U.S. In the course of the project, the Ukrainians learned that in Canada's negotiations with the U.S., Canada won 50% of the cases. The Ukrainian government often cited Canada-U.S. negotiations as examples and precedent, using Canadian negotiating techniques against the Russians, much to their chagrin. Of course, the U.S. was a civilized party to such negotiations. With the overbearing and aggressive Russians, negotiations were a different matter.

When Orest came to Kiev, the two of us would scour the city for CDs of Ukrainian folk music. After a few forays that yielded very little, I realized there was hardly any market for this genre. I suggested to Orest that I would sponsor a singer or a choir to record the most popular Ukrainian folk songs if he could find the right musicians. He introduced me to Bohdan Kuts of the Vydubichi Church Choir, a church that Hengching and I often visited for walks around the compound. I offered the choir U.S. $2,000 to help them produce a CD. They presented me with the finished CD on my birthday, February 20, 2002. This came as a complete surprise. I had invited a few people for a celebratory dinner at our house and as we were about to eat, the door swung open and in walked the Vydubichi Choir singing Ukrainian birthday songs. Volodiya, Natalia, and Liubko Markevych came up with idea and they had even told Hengching who carefully kept the plan a secret from me.

I met Lubomyr (Liubko) Markevych walking around in the historical city of Lviv in the summer of 2002. Liubko was practicing law in Edmonton and had come to Kiev in early 1991 for a three-month contract with the UNDP. He stayed on after the contract ended and when I met him, he was working on the Dnieper River clean-up project which covered Russia, Belarus and Ukraine and involved the radioactive contamination from Chernobyl. Liubko had helped with the translation of the Ukrainian folk CD brochure and I subsequently discovered that he also sang in the choir. After I'd failed to find folksong CDs, Liubko introduced me to some very good ones including a CD with songs by his erstwhile girlfriend. When we weren't searching for music, Orest, Liubko, Bohdan and I were often sampling the food in Kiev's various Chinese restaurants. These rather obscure establishments were operated by Chinese students who were in Kiev to study music (where the training was first rate and cheap). They offered reasonably good Chinese cuisine. We went to so many places that Orest said whenever he thought of Kiev, he thought of me and the Chinese restaurants.

Liubko knew a lot about Ukraine and points of interest that were off the beaten path. He knew where one could swim near Kiev in a clean tributary of the Dnieper. Once he took me on a cycling tour of the islands and introduced me to the Bykivnia Forest, east of the Kiev Metro terminus, where the KGB had dumped the bodies of Ukrainian intelligentsia who they'd shot in the dungeon under the School for Noble Giels. Thousands of bodies were dumped in secrecy, and have since remained unclaimed, disintegrating in the soil. After the collapse of the Soviet Union, Ukrainians could finally mourn this loss and they tied blue and yellow ribbons (their national colours) on trees in the forest to commemorate the victims. Many of the trees also had heart-rending photos of the faces of those who had died at the hands of the Soviet secret police.

* * *

The Ukraine posting took me to some of the more distant and bleakest corners of the country, places that still had the monumental greyness of the Soviet era permeating the land like a thick fog. The city of Lugansk is such a place, and it is also the name of the easternmost "oblast" (administrative province) in Ukraine. This oblast still leans heavily toward Russia and is home to cities like Stakhanov, named after the socialist hero Alexey Stakhanov, a Soviet version of Lei Feng - the Chinese hero of the communist People's Liberation Army. I traveled there with Volodymyr and Natalia, and in two days we visited seven Canada Fund projects (run by four NGOs), met with the mayor of Teplogirsk, and the rector of the East-Ukrainian State University. But our trip was more than a CIDA mission. And it is not enough to say that Lugansk is the easternmost Oblast of Ukraine, surrounded by Russia on three sides. In my 1977 Britannica world atlas, the city of Lugansk appears as "Voroshirovgrad," after another Soviet military commander from the area. For me, the visit was a cultural, anthropological, almost a spiritual experience - much more than just an official mission to inspect a few projects.

The propellers and the fuselage of the tired Russian aircraft that took us to Lugansk were so old that my colleagues wondered whether it would fly. I assured them that when a plane is this old, it has been used so many times that its ability to fly shouldn't be in question. In fact, this plane was a time machine that took us from Kiev to Lugansk, and back in time two decades to Soviet times. The legacy of the U.S.S.R. was palpable everywhere, in the drab Soviet style buildings, the use of the Russian language, the slogans using Soviet phrases, and the dark and dusty airport without lights (at 5 AM) or signs. The sour-faced attendants insisted on letting the passengers into the check-in lobby one at a time, slamming the door in the face of whoever was next in line.

As the door shut you could hear them muttering, "This is the regulation."

When someone asked them to speed it up because of the long line, the attendant shouted back, "I don't care! Let them wait!"

The city was littered with statues of Lenin, rusty tractors and combines in vacant lots, semi-abandoned factories and potholes everywhere (cleaned, but not filled). It was all very interesting, but also depressing, and the NGOs provided the only bright light in this Soviet era darkness.

They demonstrated so much initiative and energy that we wished there were many more of them.

We went to places where no donor had ever visited, obscure cities like Teplogirsk where we met with the mayor. He was proud of his city's history as the origin of the Stakhanovite Movement started by Stalin in 1935. Aleksey Grigorevich Stakhanov broke the world record in coal mining production. At the city limit, there was a sign announcing this fact along with a monument to the exemplary model miner built in 1935. The mayor took pains to explain that Teplogirsk should have been called Stakhanov, but that name was given to another town and Teplogirsk was shortchanged. There was a pathetic little church, and not far from there was a dingy little museum with peeling paint and a rusty roof dedicated to Stakhanov. The town's population had declined from 20,000 in 1990 to 12,500 when we visited, and of that number it seemed that 50 percent were pensioners and the rest were children. The main source of income for the residents was derived from pensions and remittances. It was hard to be optimistic. I wondered how the mayor, who had held that position for three terms since 1991, kept his sanity in light of the dire circumstances of his city.

The mayor was working with the South East Center (of Municipal and Regional Development) to train young people to organize their own NGOs, social and cultural centers, and other events to attract and keep their age group in the area. At that time, Teplogirsk did not even have an Internet connection. We told them we could help with their efforts by providing computers and an Internet connection, if they would sustain the Internet service and make it available for training and business development purposes.

We drove out of Teplogirsk past large mounds of coal sludge that Stakhanov helped to pile up from the underground coalmines. These mounds were called "terrekon," probably a combination of the Greek word for earth (terra) and cone, in reference to their conical form. There were thousands of terrekon scattered about the mines, most of which are abandoned, though some still had their elevator shafts intact. The ground underneath the entire region had been hollowed out by thousands of mines. Cities like Donetsk and others stand on hollow ground, and a few years ago a building actually sank into the ground because the cavity underneath it had collapsed into a sinkhole. When I heard about this sinking building, I had a sinking feeling that I might find myself underground the next morning.

We had a meeting at the Oblast Library for the Youth. The Russian word for youth is "yunak," pronounced the same as "eunuch." I'm glad I'm no longer a yunak. The Public Education and Legal Assistance group (PELA) was a collection of young people, who defied the corrupt and cynical system of officials, and provided legal services helping people wronged by the regime. PELA had a Canadian intern from New Brunswick who liked the work despite the hardships and the oppressive atmosphere, and he lamented the fact that his internship was ending in 8 days. PELA also played a significant advocacy role in organizing the first advisory committee to develop a statute for self-government that incorporates the delegation of authority and public consultation. They had many depressing stories to tell. For example, delegates of the Oblast Rada bought up all the copies of a paper that reported on their corrupt and abusive conduct, the local police chief confiscated all the copies of a paper reporting on police atrocities. Despite stories like this, I left feeling somewhat optimistic about this backward place. We believed that of the 760 registered NGOs in the oblast, 130 were active and 70 of them were in Lugansk city.

In Lugansk, I met Aleksandr Glubenko, the rector of the East Ukrainian National University, and even though he'd never heard of CIDA, the University had worked with the Freedom of Choice NGO under our anti-corruption project. The rector and his staff were very eager to cooperate with us. I encouraged him to work with NGOs in his area, and gave him our program outline and guidelines on how to apply for the Canada Fund, Gender Fund, and the Election Fund. The rector was so happy to see us that he even invited us into his exercise room next to his office. There, near an exercise bike, hanging on the wall was a musket known as a "Triokh-lineika" or "three-liner." This is a well-known Russian rifle widely used by snipers for its accuracy at long distances from the Civil War following the Bolshevik Revolution to World Wars I and II.

The Rector had summoned a platoon of media reporters who were recording the meeting and several journalists came to me afterwards and asked why I said democracy is not spreading fast enough in Lugansk.

Instead of answering, I asked them, "Do you need me to tell you about the amount of abuse that's going on in this area? You guys from the media have a responsibility to tell the people about what's going on."

The rector led me to an auditorium where I was asked to speak to about 100 students, in English and without an interpreter. I gave the same talk, and encouraged them to ask me questions. Unlike in Ostrogh, there were only three questions, two from teachers. I suspect this is because the students were still used to the Soviet style of education where you absorbed information without questioning it. I tried to be provocative by saying that the first duty of an intellectual is to question all assumptions and statements. I hope they heard me.

Our last visit in the area was to see families that received Canada Fund support to introduce "California worms" to their home gardens. In 2001, we gave $9,965 to the Pnagiya NGO for the purchase, transportation, and application of worms to improve soil capacity for 50 family gardens. The California worms project proved successful in helping families, mostly pensioners, materially improve the quality of their lives. The Pnagiya NGO had approached us for funding to print and disseminate information about the worm project to more farmers. It was late in the day when we arrived, so we were only able to visit two families. In both cases, the qualitative changes in their lives were remarkable, which was very uplifting to see after two long and grueling days. The families used to buy onions, tomatoes and cucumbers, but now they were the ones selling this produce. The introduction of the worms had quadrupled both families' incomes. One family used the extra income (thanks to the worms) to pay for a 10 meter well. When their neighbors, friends, and families learned of their success, they asked to join the program. At least 15 people followed each family's lead, which meant that the help we gave to the first 50 families might have benefited some 750 families around Lugansk. An initial investment of some $20,000 was now yielding a huge amount of income and immeasurable happiness to many people.

Our visit was not only enlightening for us, but it also showed them that in some small way, they were not forgotten. Our funding was so small that it was almost embarrassing, but the impacts were so much greater proportionally, that I think we achieved results that outweighed some multimillion-dollar projects. Most importantly, this kind of development cooperation was the most effective way to introduce political change, because it did not involve direct political confrontation.

* * *

In my two years of traveling throughout the Ukraine, Volodymyr and Natalia accompanied me on almost all of my trips. Their company was a great benefit not only because of their knowledge of the projects, but also because of their knowledge of the local history. Hengching came along on some of our trips, and Olga and Valentyna joined us on others, sometimes increasing our group of travellers to six. On a few occasions, we made private trips to Crimea with the Nips who came from Warsaw, and with the Shens to Uman. We also drove around Kiev to see interesting historical spots such as Mohila Askolda (King Askold's grave), the Kkosei Kapnia hospital complex built by Peter the Great, Babi Yar, the War Museum, the Bykivnia Forest, the Synagogue, the Podil, and of course the Khreshchatyk, Kiev's main thoroughfare.

I visited Crimea four times, once in 1999 with my class reunion cruise and three times when I was posted to Kiev (with the UNDP, with our friends the Nips, and once with Francoise Ducros). Historically, the Crimea had never been a part of Ukraine, but was under the Crimean Tatars whose Sultans were independent and closer to the Ottomans than to any Ukrainian kingdom. It was only after their conquest by Peter the Great and since the rule of Catherine the Great, that Crimea belonged to the Russian Empire. Then, in 1950 Khrushchev decreed Crimea to be a part of Ukraine (in part because Khrushchev was the commissar for Ukraine in the 30's). To this day, the main port of Sevastopol is still the home to the Russian Black Sea fleet, and Crimea has a significant Russian minority that identifies with Russia instead of Ukraine. In this respect, Ukraine's problems with Russia resemble Taiwan's difficulties with China, except fortunately for Ukraine the problem is not nation-wide, but limited only to Crimea and Donetsk.

During my first visit on the Taida Reunion Cruise, we visited several ports including Yalta and Odessa in Ukraine. I ended up seeing more than the tour covered, including the Alupka Palace, Lastochkino Gniezdo or the Sparrow's nest, a small palace built on the rock jutting out into the Black Sea, and the second floor of the Livadiya Palace where the Tsar had a private apartment and one could see his furniture and photos taken by Nicolas II. My second trip was in 2002, when I joined the UNDP inspections. On that trip I learned about the Turkish support of the Tatars and I saw Belagorska ("white cliff") where the Crimean Tatars held their "kurultai," an assembly of clan chiefs. My third visit to Crimea was also in 2002 with Hengching and the Nip family. In Livadiya, Hengching was more interested in the second floor royal apartment than in the main floor where the 1944 Yalta Conference took place. In the royal apartment, Nicolas II's photographs showed his family of four daughters and his son, the haemophiliac Aleksei. Hengching stood in front of these photos for a long time, lost in thought and almost in tears. Nicolas was a good man and a good father, but he was unable to deal with the growing crisis in Russia. In 1917 he inspected the navy in Sevastopol, but refrained from going to Livadiya because he did not want to enjoy the comforts of the chateau while Russian soldiers were fighting on the front.

My last trip to Crimea, organized by Volodiya in 2004, was the richest and most interesting of them all. First we went to Kherson in the eastern end of Crimea on the northernmost shores of the Black Sea. The city was once the site of an ancient Greek colony, Chersonesos, from which it derives its name. Nearby, lay the 5th century ruins of Panticapaeum, another Greek colony and the tomb of an unknown King. In an earlier trip, I'd managed to get a glimpse of a nuclear submarine in a dry dock in Balaclava, the Sultan's palace in Bakchisarai, but this time I was taken inside the inner sanctum of the former Soviet nuclear fleet. Making our way down the coast to Yalta, we stopped at Balaclava, where Volodiya managed to get us a guided tour of a Soviet nuclear submarine base deep inside a mountain cave. Descending into this cave filled us with anxiety, and this was amplified by the thought that in this complete darkness the Soviets hid some of their most deadly nuclear weapons. It was chilling to see the platforms for nuclear bombs in a cave that had once been brightly illuminated, but was now only visible by flashlight.

Not far from the submarine base was a huge rocky outcrop over an abandoned salt mine that once housed 10,000 underground fighters during the Nazi occupation. These resistance fighters emerged only at night in complete darkness, and they had built a virtual underground city. There were historic sites everywhere in Crimea and the scenery was breathtaking. As a foreigner, I found an intimacy to the place that is difficult to define; perhaps that's why I often say I must have been a Slav in an earlier incarnation. It is no wonder that the Russians covet Crimea.

Just to the west of Crimea is the oblast and seaport of Odessa, where we had a few projects that were interesting, despite some ominous undertones. One of our projects in the area involved the Filatov Eye Disease Institute that had been working with us through the Science and Technology Centre, Ukraine (STCU). Going back to 1962, the institute has been a world pioneer in laser research led by its chief, Dr. Leonid Linnik, who studied the use of lasers in curing eye diseases. Dr. Linnik achieved remarkable results in the treatment of tage-related macular dystrophy, which affects 50 million people annually worldwide, and he has even been able to reverse the damage if its extent was less than 50 percent. He has used lasers to treat glaucoma by stimulating the retina in such a way that the blockage could be corrected without drilling a hole in the eye, as many eye specialists do in North America.

Why was Dr. Linnik's institute funded by the STCU? Because the institute once had a military role during the Cold War, and Dr. Linnik conducted research in the use of the lasers as weapons to blind enemy pilots and kill enemy soldiers. From 1962 to 1991, Linnik worked with scientists from Sukumy in Georgia. His office still has a steel door to protect the top-secret research that was conducted inside. He used monkeys for experiments, and in the course of several years 1,500 monkeys were sacrificed for his research gaining him the nickname "monkey-killer."

He told us a fascinating story of meeting his American counterparts after the collapse of the USSR. The Americans were engaged in similar activities and the CIA had been collecting information about Linnik. When they met in the U.S., the Americans told Linnik that they knew all about him, and Linnik, impishly told them that he also knew all about them thanks to the diligent efforts of the KGB. So the two opposing sides had finally found each other at either end of their telescopes! Apparently, they all had a good laugh and now communicate with each other like old friends.

Some of Linnik's work was based on the idea that a laser beam's different spectra and wavelengths can affect the eye differently, so by providing different stimuli, the laser could be used to repair damage caused by diabetes, and could even help reduce the risk of cancer by stimulating the immune system. Perhaps there is something in his research that the medical/ industrial sector of Canada could benefit from through a joint venture using such technological approaches.

I visited Odessa on five different occasions, with an increasing sense of nostalgia and sadness on each trip. The city was largely built by Catherine II with the help of Count Richelieu, the French Cardinal's nephew. It thrived as a major port in the Black Sea trade, and developed a fine, genteel culture. It also had a world-class music academy that produced such talents as David Oistrakh, Sfiatoslav Richter, and many others. The Opera House of Odessa once attracted the best singers and conductors, but now it is selling season tickets for as little as $50. The Odessans are well-known for their sly humour, and every year there is an annual joke festival. Pushkin lived in Odessa for a year where he wrote two chapters of his famous novel in sonnet form, *Eugene Onegin*.

* * *

Deep in the southwest corner of Ukraine, near the borders of Poland, Slovakia, Hungary and Romania is the Ukrainian city of Uzhgorod in the Zakarpattia oblast. In some of the towns in this area, people speak Hungarian or Romanian, instead of Ukrainian. Topographically speaking, this region doesn't seem to belong to Ukraine, as it lies outside the Carpathian Mountain range that forms the natural border of southwestern Ukraine. Even the weather here belongs to the Mediterranean and Black Sea system. I asked why Uzhgorod is a part of Ukraine, when it was more geographically contiguous with Hungary and Romania. No one seemed to know for sure. Speculation ranges from events at the end of the Austro-Hungarian Empire after World War I, to the legacy of the Soviet Union, which took it from the Hungarians after World War II and then left it to the Ukrainian state that emerged after the collapse of the USSR. Some posit that the region was the result of Roosevelt's "trembling hand" when the map of Europe was redrawn at Yalta.

Austrians had built Uzhgorod's city hall in the 19th century. Like most ethnic and cultural crossroads, Uzhgorod is a polyglot place with a very complex history. The Slavs are among its earliest settlers, and their numbers greatly increased when the Mongols invaded Ukraine and took Kiev in 1240. At that time, the Slavs escaped to Zakarpattia by crossing the Carpathian Mountains in large numbers; however, they did not succeed in their flight as the Mongols also crossed over Zakarpattia. I asked the historian, Igor Ilko, who was the director of the Carpathian Foundation (to promote economic development, ethnic relations, and NGO building), how people in the region identified themselves. He said they considered themselves Zakarpatski first and Ukrainian second. Those who speak Russian, speak the old church Slavic rather than contemporary Russian, and they didn't feel any affinity to Russia or the Russian people. Interestingly, at one time Uzhgorod's population was 50 percent Jewish, and one can still visit the synagogue that stands on a prime location on the banks of Uzh.

Uzhgorod is named after the river Uzh, which means, "snake." There are several bridges that span the river and they are vulnerable to spring floods when the water gushes over them. Buildings of the Austro-Hungarian period have statues on their roofs and spires – animals, gods, and heroes. There was a statue of Saints Cyril and Methodius, inventors of the Cyrillic alphabet in the 9th century. Unlike the Georgians who invented their own alphabet, the origins of Cyrillic lie in the modified Greek alphabet. The statue stands in the central "rynok" or market of Uzhgorod, suggesting that in a region where five countries meet in what was once a predominantly non-Slavic area, the statue reinforces the strategy of Ukrainianization.

On the way from Uzhgorod to Khust, I saw a structure that looked like an abandoned apartment building and I asked Igor Ilko about it. According to Ilko, it was a missile tracking station built by the Soviets to track Tomahawk missiles from the U.S. 6th Fleet stationed in the Mediterranean. There was so much secrecy around the building that people were told it was a spaghetti factory. Apparently, the complex was constructed at a huge cost of millions, but it was abandoned and obsolete. I took some photos of the place after lunch, and it's likely that had I done so 15 years ago, the Soviet authorities would have thrown me in jail.

In the village Nizhne Selyshe we visited a cheese plant started by an NGO whose purpose was to keep the young people of the village from leaving by providing them with training, a place for recreation, cultural activities like movies and discos, and the internet. The NGO created a cheese plant that was up to international standards, and was supplied by milk collected only from farmer families at 3 to 6 liters a day. No one believed the cheese plant would survive let alone succeed, however,

they hoped to break even in the following year. At one time, the village
didn't even have clean water, and people had to fetch water from a spring
4 kilometers up a hill. It was a remarkable example of a self-starter that
survived even when the conditions were not favorable, the local authority
was unhelpful, resources were scarce, and the people were poor.

My other travels in the western part of the country took me to a
colleague's birthplace in the Carpathian Mountains near the Polish border.
I met Vira Nanivska when she was the head of International Centre for
Policy Studies (ICPS), a prominent NGO in Kiev. Vira enjoyed the trust
and confidence of many senior officials in the Ukrainian government. I
was introduced to Vira at Marvin Wodinski's place in April, 2002 when
I first came to Kiev for familiarization. After I'd settled into my posting,
Vira invited Hengching and me to her birthplace in the mountains for
a couple of days of mushroom hunting and mountain climbing, thus
giving us firsthand experience of life in the country.

About 500 kilometres east of Uzhgorod is the medieval city of
Kamianets-Podilskyi with its ancient castle built by Polish kings to defend
against Ottoman and Tatar invasions. The modern city is actually about
two kilometres from the fortress and contains many monuments that
reflect the city's cosmopolitan history. There is the university, a heritage
centre, a Polish square with a "ratusha" (town hall), an Armenian church,
a mosque, the churches of St. Paul and St. Peter, and a mosque-turned-
church that the future king of Poland, Stanislas Poniatovski, had visited
in the 18th century.

Kamianets-Podilskyi has been influenced by at least seven cultures
including Russians, Tatars, Turks, Lithuanians, Poles, Jews, and
Armenians. There is also evidence that the site's origins lie in antiquity
with the Dacians and that it was mentioned by Ptolemy and Pliny.
Nearby is a point where the rivers Dniester and Zbuchi meet marking
the location of the old border between Poland, Romania and the Soviet
Union. Until 1939, this was an international border with Poland on the
west side of the Zbuchi, the Soviet Union on the east side, and Romania
the south side of the Dniester. I stood on the bridge that once connected
Poland and the USSR and looked towards Romania. The former Polish
side is now called Okopy, the Soviet side is now Isakivchi, and the former
Romanian side is called Ataky.

While Kamianets-Podilskyi was the southernmost bastion for the Slavs from Russia and Poland, some 30 kilometers to the south is the city of Khotin, the northernmost fortress for the Ottoman Turks. The fortress is visible from the river Dniester, but it cannot be seen approaching from land, which presents the sight of a wall, but no fortress. The visitor has no idea what lies beyond the wall until they pass through the main gate when the top of the impressive fortress comes into view. Inside, there is a dungeon, living quarters for soldiers and knights, a mosque-turned-church, and a modern exhibition room displaying armor, weapons, and a statue of a leader who defeated the Turks for the last time in the early 17th century.

The city of Cherkassy lies 400 kilometers east of Kamianets-Podilskyi and was the site for a project launch that I attended with Natalia. The Cherkassy Youth Center seemed to be under the direction of an activist director with NGO participation, and the enthusiasm at the center was such that we stayed twice as long as we'd originally planned. The Oblast was very keen to implement new projects and was prepared to mobilize civil society resources to carry out project work.

We left Kiev for Cherkassy at 6 AM, and returned by 7:30 that evening. It was an exhausting trip, but my visit impressed the Oblast administrators, underscoring the importance that CIDA attached to the success of their project and strengthening their commitment. There was little time to visit any interesting historical sites such as Chyhyrin, where Bohdan Khmelnitsky was born and which served as the capital of the first Ukrainian state established by Cossacks known as the "Hetmanate." Still, on our way back we passed a monument to "the Second Front" at Korsun Khmelnitsky, where the Soviet Army under Koniev, Malinovsky and Vatutin destroyed six Nazi divisions in January 1944.

* * *

Just as Kherson and Kamianets-Podilskyi were once Greek settlements in antiquity, Olvia was also established by the Greeks in 600 B.C. Herodotus visited the city on the northern shore of the Black Sea in the 5th century B.C. I learned of a theory, strongly disputed by most scholars who revere Herodotus as the father of history that Pericles asked for a report to help persuade the Athenians of the need and feasibility of colonizing the Black Sea littoral areas. Apparently, Athens and other

Greek city-states were becoming dangerously dependent on grain from these areas. Olvia thrived for over 1000 years, until it was completely destroyed by the Huns in 370 A.D. The emergence of the Samatians in 300 BC had already started to weaken its hold in the area. Now there are only ancient ruins, but it was an eerie feeling to stand on the cliff overlooking the Black Sea at the mouth of the Bug River. I imagined how lonely and precarious it must have felt for the Greeks two thousand years ago to find themselves in such a distant land surrounded by 'barbarians.' As I stood there at the site of a ruined temple looking out over the Black Sea, I watched a ship sailing away in the distance, and I felt the wonder and poetry at the sight of a modern cargo ship sailing past an ancient seaport.

Our 72 year-old guide, August Ernestovich Birlych, was both well informed and very funny. He said he'd suffered three years imprisonment in a Nazi concentration camp, but I had my doubts. He would have been 14 years old at the end of World War II, but he had not lost his zest for life, even after eight tough years under Stalin. August was a remarkable man, and he shared his knowledge of Olvia with us in great detail. However, he did not know about Scyles, the Scythian prince who was executed by Scythian tribesmen for betraying his traditions and joining the Dionysian festival at Olvia. A ring bearing the name Scyleo was discovered near the mouth of the Danube in the 90s, and was authenticated as belonging to Scyles. I remember there was a spring from which the ancient citizens of Olvia took their water that was still running and drinkable today.

On another work-related trip, Volodymyr, Natalia and I visited the towns of Drohobych, Halych and Chernivtsi traveling from the western end of Ukraine to its southern oblast, Chernivtsi, on the Romanian border. Drohobych is a very old river port dating from 1114 when a wooden city wall had been built around a nearby monastery. It was also an important centre of learning, and we were taken to the statue of Yurii Kotormak Drohobych, a mathematician and astronomer who was Copernicus's teacher in Krakow. Kotormak is reputed to have calculated the movements of the solar system and accurately predicted a solar eclipse. His face reminded me of the composer Franz Liszt.

Halych is another old port city near the Dniester. The Kievan Russ King Danilo Drohobych reigned here in the 13th century after uniting western Ukraine with Kiev and Pereyaslav. I think he was also the king who built many defensive fortifications against the Mongols, only to be forced to dismantle them by the Mongols. Near the church dating from 1367 is an underground fireplace, which I suspect may be the site of a Zoroastrian sacred fire worship site, though I am not sure either Persians or Indian Parsees ever set foot there.

* * *

One of the NGO contacts who became a friend was Serhyi Maksimenko, and I will never forget his astute observation on Ukrainian civil society. Serhyi remarked that "it was no longer safe for Ukrainian politicians to take the stupidity of the populace for granted." He was speaking in reference to the elections that led to the Orange Revolution, elections that amply proved the truth of his observation. As my posting in Kiev neared its end, I began to feel sad about leaving friends like Serhyi, Bohdan Kravchenko and Liubko Markevych.

Just before my departure from Kiev, I was asked to host the Regional Representatives' Meeting for CIDA. Volodiya and Natalia organized the venue, and Olga Brizhan, our secretary, worked so hard and efficiently that there were no glitches. She was so busy that virtually nobody saw her except for those who asked her for help. So when the Senior VP was making a presentation on agency strategy, I interrupted him when Olga entered the room.

"Excuse me Rick, I must interrupt you for one minute. This is Olga, our secretary. If all of you had no problems with your hotel room, transportation, and emails, it is because of Olga's hard work. I feel that we owe her some acknowledgement for her good work. She is so busy that you rarely see her, so I thought I would take this opportunity to introduce her. Please give her an applause." There was a standing ovation, and Rick, the Senior VP, was very pleased, as was Olga.

At the end of the meeting, we organized a "wheels-up" dinner party. I was tired, and decided to give it a pass. Natalia phoned Hengching who persuaded me that we should go to the party. I should have had a clue about what lay in store for me, but I didn't. When we arrived the entire CIDA crew of some fifty people stood up and gave me a standing ovation. Volodiya and Natalia, Valentyna and Olga had conspired to turn the "wheels-up" party into my farewell party, with the entire CIDA crew from the region in attendance to wish me a happy retirement.

When I had decided to retire after only two years, Volodiya, Natalia, Valentyna, and Olga all protested and asked me to reconsider. I was touched, but I thought the Program deserved someone who was not afflicted with ALS. They talked to Francoise Ducros, and she also asked me to reconsider, even though by this time my successor had been announced. I said it was not my desire to leave. In fact, I would have liked to stay for five years if I could. My decision was based on my belief that to do justice to the dedication and commitment of the local staff, Kiev needed a program leader who was not ill.

18

THE REPUBLICS: ARMENIA, GEORGIA, UZBEKISTAN, AND AZERBAIJAN

While I was posted in Kiev, I had two projects that took me outside the country to four of the newly independent republics. I traveled to Georgia, Uzbekistan, and Azerbaijan to attend the Governing Board meeting for STCU, and to Armenia to attend the training session of the Center for Trade, Policy, and Law (CTPL).

The annual review of the project supporting the World Trade Organization's (WTO) accession efforts in Ukraine, Armenia, Georgia, and Russia took place in Yerevan, Armenia, with Carleton University's CTPL acting as the executing agency. Senior government officials, think-tank members, academics, and NGO workers were all in attendance. The project provided training on trade policy formulation, trade laws (harmonization with WTO regulations), and the development of CTPLs as centers of excellence in research, training, policy development, and trade negotiation.

It was my first (and last) visit to Yerevan. We stayed at the Hotel Yerevan in the city center, and as was my habit, I took a walk around the city as soon as I checked into the hotel. The Armenians were in the process of replacing Cyrillic with the English alphabet so street signs were half in English and half in Armenian. Next to my hotel was the Moskva Theatre with a bas-relief portrait of Lenin on its wall. In a twist of supreme poetic justice, the theater was showing the "Passion of Christ" at the time. The Opera House in Yerevan is large and opulent, and after the CTPL meetings we went to see Armenian folk dancing. The tune, rhythm, and the instruments felt very much like Aram Khachaturian's "Sword Dance." Khachaturian's seated statue adorned the front of the Opera House.

Armenia boasts the "oldest church in Christendom," that is independent from both Rome and Byzantium, and has its own Catholicos (Pope). This independence contributed to the fierce pride of the Armenians, but it also cost them dearly throughout their history. Surrounded on all sides by Turkey, Iran, and Azerbaijan – all Muslim neighbors – Armenia had spent more than a thousand years fighting off the Muslims (and often failing). None of the Christian kingdoms, near or far, came to their assistance, because the Armenians refused to swear allegiance to either the Roman Catholic Pope or the Eastern Orthodox Church. One result of Armenia's encounters with its Muslim neighbors is that it has been influenced by their Islamic cultures in the folk costume, dancing style, folksongs, and even their cuisine. Interestingly, Armenian facial features seem far more Central Asian than European.

One of the CTPL participant institutions, the Yerevan State University, hosted a dinner showcasing fantastic Armenian cuisine.

I made a toast on behalf of CIDA, "I would like to toast the old culture of Armenia. Where else do you have the statue of a mythical hero like David of Sassun adorning the Yerevan Railway Station?"

We were taken to the Manuscript Library where they have fascinating, very old historical documents, watched over by a stone statue of Saint Mesrob Mashtots, the 4th century monk who invented the Armenian alphabet. The manuscripts were made of parchment and its authors had frequently painted new text over an existing text, presumably because parchment was scarce. Some of their past owners had buried many of the manuscripts for centuries, in order to preserve them from destruction at the hands of Muslim and Mongol invaders. The books came in different materials, sizes, and shapes. There were several written on palm-leaves that looked very much like the Buddhist sutras one finds in Tibet and Sri Lanka. Then there were tiny books, 11th century calendars measuring three by four centimeters, and astronomical essays from 13th century based on the Ptolemaic theory of universe with the earth at its centre. Echmiadzin, the seat of the Catholicos (head of the Armenian Church) is the equivalent to their version of the Vatican. Armenian holy orders do not report to anyone else because they are completely independent. It is a tribute to their stubbornness that the Armenian Church is still going strong all over the world. The Cathedral gives one a false impression of being small when, in fact, it is quite large. The beautiful and vivid colors inside emphasize reds, blues, and gold, and the main entrance gate reminded me of the finest Mughal architecture in India.

According to a tradition that goes back to time immemorial, all churches, tombs, and holy sites must have a "khachkar," a carved wood or stone stele with a cross and floral designs. I asked the curator of the Echmiadzin Treasury how Armenian khachkar differed from the crosses found in other churches. It was a simple and innocent question, but it elicited a very interesting answer. First, he said that the Armenian cross does not have the body of Christ, because they believe the body is transient and that it was on the cross for only a few hours. Further, Armenian Christians believe the cross symbolizes eternal life transcending terrestrial confinement. There is no Latin inscription of "INRI" (Iesus Nazarenus Rex Indaeorum or "Jesus of Nazareth, King of the Jews") on top of the cross. He said that the Latin inscription was an insult because Christ was God, Lord of the universe, not just King of the Jews. He said there is nothing to show St. Andrew at the foot of the cross, because the cross belongs to Christ alone, and there is no crescent at the foot of the cross symbolizing the crushing of the Islam because the cross is not a weapon. Finally, the cross has eight tips, symbolizing eight nations.

* * *

Armenian brandy is renowned for its quality throughout the world. It was reported that during the Yalta Conference of 1944, Churchill specifically requested Armenian brandy as his after-dinner drink. I visited a factory that makes this famous brandy and saw the manufacturing process first-hand. At the factory, I remember I was actually able to tell the difference in quality as I was given a tasting of progressively better grades of brandy. Of the four categories of Armenian brandy, I can only remember "Akhtamara," the second best. Perhaps because the name Tamara was either related to a famous queen, or to a young girl whose lover drowned when he lost his way swimming to her.

He was said to utter, "Akh Tamara, I love you," before he drowned. Anyway, I assure you the brandy was superb.

Mount Ararat was supposed to be visible from Yerevan, but it was hidden behind a thick curtain of cloud the entire time I was there. Finally, as my plane was taking off from the capital, I saw a spectacular view of Mount Ararat emerging from the cloud. Stunned, I took out my camera and got some breathtaking photos of the famous mountain and of the snow-covered Caucasus Mountains from the window of my Tupolev.

* * *

We arrived in Tbilisi, Georgia four and a half hours late because Aerosvit, the Ukrainian airline, had failed to pay for fuel and the plane was unable to take off. I missed a dinner date with Olga Bondar of the Dutch NGO Press Now, but Olga came to my hotel to say good night.

When I apologized for being so late, she said "So what?"

It's people like Olga who work in the development sector that makes me feel good to belong to their kind.

I visited Tbilisi to inaugurate a multi-donor project (U.S., Canada, E.U.) that gave grants to former Soviet weapons scientists to research peaceful (and commercially profitable) applications of technology. This was part of the nuclear safety effort, trying to keep these scientists gainfully employed so they don't end up going to Iraq, North Korea, or other dangerous regimes. So far, we have spent more than $50 million over the last four years on this project, and some of the results are not only interesting, but also potentially lucrative. I never knew that Georgia was home to so many world-class scientists, and in the three short days I was there, I visited several institutes that produced incredible goods, which if properly marketed, could bring in huge revenues. The problem is that scientists are not businessmen, and our project aimed at not only providing them with grants to conduct research, but also to help them find international firms for investment.

Quite unexpectedly we were invited to meet with President Shevardnadze who spoke with us for just under an hour. I told Shevardnadze that Georgians were well liked by Ukrainians, and that in the centre of Kiev there was a street called "Shota Rustaveli Street," in honor of the Georgian national poet, from the 12th Century. I said that, on a personal note, I'd been an admirer of his since the Gorbachev days when he presided over Glasnost and Perestroika. I was also a relief that he did not invade the Baltic countries when they declared their independence.

"History will remember you." I said – How's that for being ingratiating?

He seemed well pleased by my comments. I thought he was making eye contact with me during most of the meeting, even though our delegation consisted of three persons and I had deliberately told my project manager to take the centre seat. Maybe Shevardnadze could not quite believe that I was a Canadian diplomat, and not Japanese or Korean, (even though I gave him my card with the Maple Leaf prominently displayed).

During our meeting with the President, Shevardnadze recommended that we visit the Institute of Stable Isotopes that had several contracts and investors from the U.S. and Germany. The institute had published papers in the British Medical Journal and the New England Journal of Medicine, and had caught the attention of several American pharmaceutical companies that subsequently invested in further research into commercially marketable products. For example, boron 10, carbon 13, oxygen 17 and 18, and nitrogen 13 all have medical applications, boron 11 can be used for microelectronics, and silicon 28 is useful for semiconductors.

Dr. Nina Khuchua, director of the institute, had a lab that made high quality wafers for Intel. The lab had to be dust free and it had recently received a donation of second-hand equipment from Germany. The lab required assistance to install and calibrate the equipment and I didn't understand why the Germans hadn't given them full assistance. Dr. Khuchua told me that the machines were made in the U.S., and unfortunately, the German aid office could not finance a technical expert from the U.S. Maybe our project might be able to help.

Our schedule was quite full and because of the meeting with Shevardnadze, our original arrangements were thrown into disarray. We hardly had time to have lunch. Still, I managed to get up early in the morning to take a walk around the hotel. Members of OSCE and the World Bank in Kiev warned me that I should be careful not to walk alone while it was dark outside. I walked anyways, and my overall impression was that the place was quite peaceful and the people were very friendly, not threatening at all.

Tbilisi looks like a combination of a caravanserai, a frontier town, and a medium-sized middle-European city - sort of a cross between Kiev and Kabul. Ancient fortresses, walled communities, and old churches were everywhere - downtown, in the suburbs, and on the banks of the Mktvari River (also known as the Kura). The streets were lined with monolithic, Soviet-style buildings and quaint old shops selling antiques, and there were even a few Internet cafes here and there. I noticed a visible effort to introduce English, which appeared on most signs including those on government buildings such as state museums or ministries. English has taken the place of Russian. Most of the private enterprises in Tbilisi, including the restaurants, casinos, banks, bookstores, art galleries, and tourist agencies all had their signs in Georgian and English. The Georgian script is unique, and I am told that in the former Soviet Union, there were only three nationalities with unique scripts, the other two being Armenian and Russian. But Russians took their alphabet from the Greeks, so maybe there are really only two.

Georgians were especially proud of their legendary wines, of which the Tsinandali is one of the best. We visited the Tsinandali winery, located in an abandoned gypsum mine and sampled some of the vintage wines in their cellars. There were three bottles that remained of the 1841 vintage that were, of course, no longer drinkable, but still kept sealed as a historical relic. At the Tsinandali winery we were served lunch with several red and white wines, all of which were quite good. They say the Georgian wines are so fine and well known that there are many fakes to be found in Ukraine and Poland. The prices were not at all high, ranging from $3 to $15 a bottle. I brought home two bottles, which I enjoyed later.

When you visit a friend in the Kakheti region, you must sample their homemade wine. They store it in underground cisterns, and serve it in a horn that is lowered into the cistern like a bucket to retrieve the wine. Prof Kvistadze took us to his friend near South Ossetia where we were taken to the room with an underground cistern for wine. Sure enough, his friend lowered a horn through a hole in the ground to get the wine. The wine was so good, that the visitor could be forgiven for thinking that the cistern looked more like an outhouse than a wine well.

Georgian food is also very popular in Poland and Ukraine, and I was fortunate enough to sample some excellent cuisine in two restaurants in Tbilisi. The Marco Polo restaurant was fantastic and the décor was also beautiful. On two occasions, we had no time for a full lunch, so we went to two different fast-food places and even they served very tasty fare at incredibly low prices. In between meals and travel for work, I also managed to sneak in a few minutes for carpet shopping and I ended up purchasing a dark brown kilim rug.

* * *

We had an opportunity to leave Tbilisi and visit the northeastern frontier region of Kakheti. This area is a few miles from Chechnya, and I was told that Chechen marauders sometimes wandered across the Caucasus Mountains that separate the two states. The mountains looked absolutely forbidding - snow bound, rocky and steep - and I had a hard time imagining how one could simply cross over as though it were part of a routine. As we approached the Chechen border, the vista of the Caucasus Mountains and their towering, craggy ranges was both majestic and mythic. I felt something similar to this in India when I saw the Himalayas up close. Of course, the Himalayas were much larger than the Caucasus and so were even more imposing, more awe-inspiring and overwhelming. But both times, I felt that I was so close, I could reach out and touch the mountains with my hands.

During the three-hour drive out of town, I was struck by the austere landscape and the fortifications that dotted almost all the main peaks along the way. These forts were like witnesses to Georgian history, and they seemed to tell the story of a country that had been scarred by countless invasions and conquests by many outsiders including the Scythians, Samatians, Iranians, Turks, Mongols, and finally, by the Russians. There were even some fortifications built around the churches that we visited, with strong walls topped by parapets. Throughout their arduous history, the Georgian spirit remained unconquered even though their country was occupied and ruled by so many different invaders.

Georgians seemed to lack any inferiority complex, and they had not lost their native goodness at heart. The hospitality we experienced at the home of one of the Georgian scientists was simple, genuine, and warm. Our host toasted our health, our visit, our families, our children, our friends in Canada, our friendship, and the joy of being together. The Georgian songs were a bit like a cross between the Hungarian Czardas and Mongol dances. I suspect there is also a trace of their nomadic ways still flowing through their blood.

Georgians practice Orthodox Christianity, and they are generally conservative and have very long life spans (perhaps because they drink such excellent red wine). I saw a headstone of a priest's grave outside of Tbilisi in the monastery of Ninotsminda that claimed the priest had lived for 120 years! We visited several churches ranging in date from the 5th to 13th centuries such as the Church of the Holy Cross about 30 minutes drive from Tbilisi and the fortified Church of the Sacred Pillar. Some had been sacked, but the frescos in the ruined apses, many of them originals, resembled those in Kiev and even in Warsaw. One reason why Georgians feel they are part of Europe is that throughout their history, despite surviving under Russian rule for several centuries, they found an affinity not with Moscow or St Petersburg, but with the cultures of the Byzantines and Greeks.

* * *

We traveled to Tashkent, Uzbekistan to discuss STCU's role in finding a way to help former weapons-scientists engage in peaceful and commercially useful research. My contention has been to persuade others that the issue is about threat reduction, a goal that motivated the creation of STCU in the first place. If we believe the need for threat-reduction will persist beyond the end of donor contributions, then donors should be interested in enabling STCU-type activities to continue beyond the end of funding. I suggested that the best way to see that happen would be to enable the Partnership Program (funded by commercial entities and not by donors) to grow. The Partnership Program could ultimately replace donor funding and enable STCU, or its successor body to continue engaging former weapons scientists. This should all be done while STCU is still maintained by donors (and with Ukrainian Government support).

During our trip, we visited several scientific institutes and I was surprised and impressed by the high level of Uzbekistan's scientific research.

We visited the rather gloomy 10-megawatt nuclear reactor at the Institute of Nuclear Physics, a world-class physics research institution. The director of the institute said we could take photos. It was an eerie feeling to be standing in the heart of one of the former key institutions that built Soviet nuclear weapons, even when after it had fallen on hard times and required donor funding. This was the facility that made the micro nuclear reactor for the Soviet satellite that crashed in Canada in 1978. At the gate of the Institute of Nuclear Physics, a new sign in blue tiles says "Mirnyi Atom" or "Peaceful Atom," in a somewhat incongruous combination of the Uzbek mosaic tradition and capitalist marketing strategy coming together on an imposing Soviet-era gate.

At the solar furnace of the Institute of Physics there were 250 mirrors, each computer-calibrated to reflect the rays of the sun into a concave dish, which in turn focused the light into a furnace, and raising its temperature to over 2,700 degrees Celsius. An amazing feat when you consider that the surface of the sun is 6,000 degrees Celsius, and that after traveling so many million miles, its light only loses 50% of its heat. The entire impressive structure is located about an hour's drive outside of Tashkent on a hill with a breath-taking view.

We also visited Institute of Bio-organic Chemistry that conducts research on pheromones, the female hormones in insects that attract the males. Sometimes, pheromones are used to trap and kill male insects. The institute is also an authority on poisons from snakes and spiders (including the black widow) and their use in impregnating cottonseeds to kill the insects that feed on them. The cottonseeds are subsequently detoxified so the cotton, cotton oil and cake can be used for human and animal consumption. Apparently, over 70% of the cotton produced in Uzbekistan now uses this form of pesticide. I was also told that Uzbekistan is the world's fourth largest cotton producer.

I managed to meet with a few NGOs to discuss the civil society issues facing businessmen, expatriate residents, and U.S. embassy people, including the ambassador himself. The picture that emerges is very depressing, as bad as or worse than the various reports describe. But the curious thing is that the people of Uzbekistan appeared happy, or at least cheerful. Perhaps, as Aznavour, the French- Armenian chanteur sang, "Misere est moins penible au soleil" (misery is less painful in the sun). Therein lies the real, metaphysical problem that all of us must ponder in the darkness. Is it our business to "improve" the lot of others, or should we leave them to their own devices (and sovereignty)? The task of "awakening" these people against their wishes - they could not have such wishes when they are not even aware of their deprivation - has been a task often taken on by self-appointed saviors and civilizers throughout history, from Alexander the Great to Confucius and Mohammed, to the missionaries and colonizers. Unfortunately, the "saviors" are often arrogant and they also have a thankless job, as we see today in Iraq. Sadly, one fool can ask more questions than many wise men can answer.

Outside of our heavy work schedule, I managed to take a weekend and visit Bukhara. Uzbekistan reminded me of Afghanistan, which I visited five times in the mid-1970s as a new CIDA officer. Even the features of the people are similar to those of Afghans. The infrastructure leaves something to be desired, and on top of that, there is a strong legacy of the Soviet "culture." Service at the airport was very nice, simply because they received instructions from their Cabinet of Ministers to be nice to us, and the Intercon in Tashkent and the Afrasiab in Samarkand were also nice, and for the same reason. But despite these pleasant encounters, there were dark spots where the Soviet legacy poked through. For example, I wanted to exchange U.S. $100, but the ladies at the Exchange Office told me there was "no money." It was noon, so I could not believe I was too early or too late. When I asked when they would have money, they said tomorrow. The next day, I wanted to be on the safe side so I had $200 exchanged, and you should have seen the piles of money I received in exchange. The notes all came in denominations of 100 SUM, which is equivalent to 10 cents U.S. I had prepared a wallet, but I ended up using a laundry bag to carry away the two thousand notes. The incredible thing was that when I paid for the hotel in local currency, they counted every note! The Intercon is a curious combination of Soviet-style service and capitalist rip-off. It cost 120 SUM or 12 cents U.S. postage to mail a postcard to North America.

At the Intercon, the concierge said, "No problem. Give us the card and we will mail it for you. The fee for this service is 500 SUM."

One important difference between Uzbekistan and Afghanistan was that the Uzbeks did not seem too hung-up on religion. Even in the villages that we passed on our way to Samarkand and Bukhara, I rarely saw any women in veils, never mind burkhas. I read somewhere that the Uzbeks are genuinely confident of their culture, and would prefer to keep their distance from the Russians, whom they secretly look down upon. There is a very strong desire to learn English, and the official policy was to replace Cyrillic with Latin script by 2005. I was told the younger generation does not understand Russian any more, and that they are all learning English or other Western European languages. Another difference between Uzbekistan and Afghanistan is that there are first-rate scientists in Uzbekistan. My STCU colleagues, including the science advisers were very impressed by what they encountered. The institutes of nuclear physics, bioorganic chemistry, zoology and the solar energy institute were all conducting fascinating research, evident even to a non-scientist like me.

* * *

Tashkent, the capital of Uzbekistan, is a major city with a population somewhere between 2 and 4 million people. Nobody knows for certain exactly how many people live there. Like most metropolises, there were several modes of public transportation and I took them all – bus, subway, and tram. In spite of its seedy appearance, the tram was quite efficient, and my adventurous spirit suitably impressed my colleagues. Of course, I was only trying to save time and energy from having to walk 10 kilometers. I took a photo in Tashkent's subway and almost immediately two police officers approached me demanding to see my "aparata" (camera). I had a regular camera in my bag in case my digital camera failed, so I gave it to them and told them, in English, that I was a guest of their president.

They duly returned the camera and said sternly, "No photo."

"Da, Da…"

So now I am the proud owner of a rare shot of the forbidden subway station next to the Intercon Hotel in Tashkent.

In another encounter with the authorities, this time at the border between Uzbekistan and Kazakhstan, I took a photo of the border guards and the barrier before the guards could say no. When they raised their hands, I put away my camera and this seemed to have satisfied them. I think it is often more a matter of proving who the boss is, and not out of any real concern with security.

The Tashkent Opera House was built in the fifties, largely by slave labor from Japanese prisoners of war. While I was in town, I went to see Donizetti's Lucia di Lammermoor. It wasn't a bad performance, but the house was only about 20% full. The incongruity of the whole evening was a little overwhelming and sad. Imagine listening to an Italian opera that is based on a work by Walter Scott and is set in Scotland, but performed inside a building built in a land entirely foreign to Italian opera built by Japanese slave labor on Stalin's orders! And my ticket cost only $1.50. How do they survive?

The longing for water is congenital and common to all people who live in arid lands including the "Stans." It also manifests itself in the blue domes of mosques and other buildings of central Asia. In one of the city's many mosques, I saw an English sign that said, "May a good mood always follow you." It was part of a come-on for a puppet show. The puppeteer was very pleasant and invited me to go inside "for a cup of tea." Then he tried to sell me a puppet for U.S. $50. They were probably not worth more than $2, so I just thanked him and left. Tashkent was not an expensive place. At the roadside shashlik (kebab) stand by the road next to the bazaar, three of us ate several shashliks, with tea and bread, and the entire meal cost us 1,200 SUM, or U.S. $1.20.

* * *

There was a UNICEF project training carpet makers in Bukhara that brought us to that ancient trading post along the fabled Silk Route. Inhabited for over five millennia, the Tajiks form the largest group in the city with ethnic Uzbeks, Russians, and Armenians comprising the rest of the population. Bukhara has long been a major centre of carpet weaving with a design specific to the city, the famous Bukhara, or "elephant foot" pattern. However, since the relatively recent period of Soviet control, the city has lost the fine art of carpet weaving, and the UNICEF project was an attempt to revive that tradition. Bukhara reflects a strange mix of modern and ancient architecture, beautiful blue-tiled mosques and the same plain houses and walls of mud and straw that are typical of the old quarters found in all central Asian cities.

My recollections of the city are a mixture of fragmentary details. I remember being accosted by a pretty girl selling pouches at a souvenir stand in the Silk Road Crossroad Pavilion. After my colleague purchased a pouch from her, she asked me to take a photo of her and I obliged her. I remember the very elegant, high-platform clogs on display at the old Palace in Bukhara. Apparently even within the palace compound, not all the paths were paved so this footwear was a necessity on rainy days.

I thought Muslims were supposed to be buried in unmarked graves - from dust to dust and all - and I thought their mausoleums were built not following the wishes of the dead, but by the desire of the living to commemorate the dead for posterity (as in the case of Timur and other leaders). Obviously, vanity wins again. There was a huge cemetery in Bukhara where only the rich and powerful have family plots. Apparently, the injunction to be buried in an unmarked grave is hard to ignore. Bodies are interred in underground chambers, directly below the cenotaphs, and wrapped in shrouds. At the entrance to one of the burial chambers, our guide told me a rather morbid story of how she had once crawled into a chamber and found human bones scattered about.

* * *

Samarkand is the second largest city in Uzbekistan and was once the capital of Timur's (Tamerlane's) empire in the 14th century. It is another important stop on the Silk Route and the modern road to Samarkand is lined with beautiful flowers planted along the highway divider. We stopped for lunch half way between Tashkent and Samarkand, where we were traveling to for a meeting of the governing board. Our stop was a teahouse known as a "chaikhana," a Silk Route remnant that is the essentially the same from Xinjiang, China through all the "Stans," and across central Asia. Chaikhana are charming and comfortable, and we enjoyed a hearty meal of shashlik, naan bread, and tea for about a dollar under a trellis of grape vines that provided some much welcome shade.

The mausoleum of Timur in Samarkand had been recently restored when we saw it, and it was almost back to its original grandeur. Still, it was sad to see grass already growing on top of the great blue dome. Deep within the mausoleum lay the remains of the Emperor, his two sons and grandsons. A black marble cenotaph marks his last resting place. The glory of Timur's empire lasted only a few decades, and it left behind these sad, yet sumptuous epitaphs for posterity to ponder the futility of conquests. He died from a stroke just before the planned launch of a major offensive against China. Had he not died then, I wonder if he would have succeeded in defeating the Chinese. Ming China was at the height of its power under the Yong-le emperor. The Chinese ruler had defeated the Mongols and sent a naval expedition of several hundred ships and 50,000 soldiers to extract tribute from kingdoms in Vietnam, Malaysia, Indonesia, Thailand, Ceylon, and even as far as Madagascar.

* * *

I went to Baku, the capital of Azerbaijan on the eastern coast of the Caspian Sea for another STCU Governing Board meeting to provide grants and research alternatives to former Soviet weapons scientists. Fortunately for me, the flight schedule was such that I had to spend seven days in Baku, with only three days of meetings and visits to scientific institutes. Unfortunately for me, I was sick for three days (beware of the pickles and the fish from the Caspian Sea).

The atmosphere of Baku was surprisingly cosmopolitan and Islam in Azerbaijan seems to be quite relaxed. We saw very few women with their heads covered, and restaurants did not hesitate in serving beer and wine, but not pork. There appeared to be a more money around because of the oil. The people were very friendly and they remind me of Armenians. I still wonder why such nice people like the Azeris and the Armenians should fight like cats and dogs. Reflecting a long tradition of good business practices established since ancient Silk Route times, the merchants' behaviour in Baku was honest, rational, and businesslike. They did not try to rip you off. I bought some water and paid in bills that were of the wrong denomination and the vendor returned the difference. At restaurants, waiters were very helpful in suggesting appropriate dishes, and on one occasion they even told us that we'd ordered too much food for our group.

I went carpet shopping twice, once with a Canadian colleague, and another time with an American colleague. The Azeris have fine and beautiful carpets and their asking prices were very reasonable. There was no pressure to bargain vigorously for a fair price. After being shown dozens of rugs, we settled on two and my Canadian friend asked me what I thought about an asking price of $200 a carpet.

I responded in French, "Perhaps 250 for the two," hoping the carpet seller would not understand.

He pre-empted our communication and responded in impeccable French, "240."

We were surprised, but in the end, we got what we wanted. Carpet shopping in Baku was not the same as in Istanbul where they start with outrageously inflated opening prices. You bargain the price down to 10% and somehow, you still feel cheated when the merchant agrees. Of course, the Turks have always prided themselves on being warriors rather than merchants.

One of the biggest surprises was the discovery that Azeris have abandoned Cyrillic script and adopted the Latin alphabet, which is evident from almost all of the street signs and billboards. Azerbaijan consciously wants to be out of the Russian sphere of influence. They hate the Russians for siding with the Armenians on Nagorno-Karabakh, a region in the south Caucasus that is disputed by Armenia. I tried out my lousy Russian and found that the young Azeris had lost the language, but were picking up English. On a visit to Gobustan, 70 kilometres south of Baku, to view stone-age rock drawings of horses, cows, and people, I ran into a group of soldiers and their officer. The officer spoke Russian, but none of the soldiers, aged between 17 and 19 did, although one could speak some English. I thought it was a pity that they are losing their Russian, and in the process also losing a rich cultural connection with Russia. Of course, from the Azeri point of view, Russian and English are equally foreign, and they may have decided English was the better option in order to gain the benefits of globalization.

Walking around the streets of Baku I felt quite safe. I wanted to find out how the NGOs were doing to promote human rights and democracy under very difficult conditions. I was going to ask the U.S. embassy to put me in touch with some of their contacts, but then I got sick. Nonetheless, when I was walking around Old Baku, I found signs for "The Fund of Aid for Youth," and "Eurasian International Development Association" and the like. In each case, I walked in and spoke to the people working there. Most of them concentrated on anti drug, employment, and cultural issues, nothing that was really politically sensitive. I found the UNHCR office by coincidence when I saw their vehicle parked outside. I met with their representative, Mr. Bohdan Nahajlo, a British citizen of Ukrainian descent. It was interesting to learn that there were more than 10,000 "asylum seekers," and some 78% of them are Chechens and another 15% from Afghanistan. Nahajlo told me that the pro-democracy NGOs were under great pressure.

At the American Ambassador's reception for the Governing Board, I met the Japanese Chargé d'affaires who spoke Persian and could communicate with the locals. He told me the media was less oppressed than many thought, and that journalists weren't necessarily arrested or beaten up for publishing articles critical of the government. But there might be other forms of harassment such as cutting funds and most media outlets were either state-owned or under heavy public subsidies. It seems to me that Azeris may be more interested in commercial activities if their government left them alone on that score. If you did not know what was going on as a tourist, then the lack of democracy would not seem especially oppressive. Huge billboards with the late President Aliev's portrait are everywhere, but somehow they appear more comical than authoritarian or depressing. Maybe Azeris see him as a father figure? The general consensus was that intellectuals were pushing for more democracy and complaining about state strong-arm tactics primarily because they are most vulnerable to the raw force of the state.

I liked Baku a lot more than Tashkent. For one thing, it was more scenic than the oil town that I'd expected to visit. There is a surprisingly large number of Western European style buildings built around 1900 by the oil tycoons of the day. There was even an exact replica of the Monte Carlo Opera House that now serves as the Philharmonic House. Most of these tycoons were shot by the Soviets. The boulevard along the Caspian Sea, Nefchilar Street, was so named after the Azeri word for the petroleum that had made Baku rich in modern industrialized times, resembles the French Riviera or Nice. Azerbaijan depends on oil for much of its economic wealth and this is unlikely to change unless tourism picks up and the carpet business is re-discovered.

Of course, a distinctly Islamic influence could also be felt in the style of some of Baku's architecture. Even some of the western buildings had onion domed corner towers suggestive of minarets. And then there is the Old City with its 14th century wall, and its towers and fortresses left by past Islamic kingdoms. We visited the Maiden Tower that forms a part of the old city wall and appears, from an aerial perspective, like a key. The tower did not get its name from any romantic story about a maiden and her lover as in Romeo and Juliet. The tower got its name after a ghastly tale about a jealous husband who threw his wife from its heights after wrongly accusing her of infidelity. The guide told us another version in which the tower gets its name for never having been taken by enemies, thus remaining inviolate like a metaphorical virgin. The spectacular view from the top sweeps across the Caspian Sea on one side to the Old City on the other. Most of the carpet merchants have their shops in this neighbourhood, so if you want to shop for carpets in Baku just tell your taxi driver to go to the Maiden Tower.

Other signs of Islam included incongruities like the pavilions for people to wash their hands and faces in the middle of very western looking streets. Mosques are present, but not everywhere suggesting that the Azeri Islamic tradition is very much in harmony with modern, secular life. I asked our guide, who was also running an NGO critical of the government, how much fundamentalism there was in Azerbaijan and he replied with a contemptuous snicker, "Zero."

As we drove through the Old City, we passed a building that appeared especially distinguished in its elegance. The driver simply said three letters, "KGB." I returned to the place the next day to have a better look. There were two armed guards standing in front of the main gate. I approached with a big smile, and asked if I could take a photo of them. They shied away, so I took a photo of the building instead, although I wish I could've taken their photo. I still remember how they looked like Mongolian warriors armed with Kalashnikovs, helmets, and bandoleers. Just down street was the Office of Marriage Registration built in 1912 by one of the oil millionaires who were undoubtedly shot by the predecessors of the people occupying the building with the guards.

Dr. Yatskiv took me to a market to buy caviar that cost only $15 per can, much cheaper than in Ukraine where I am told it would cost US$30. As I am not a great fan of caviar, I declined to purchase the delicacy. I always thought the Caspian Sea was the largest body of fresh water, but near the sea there is considerable salt production, so I must be wrong - the Caspian is a saltwater lake. My guide, Dr. Yatskiv, was a highly respected Academician from the Ukrainian National Academy of Sciences. The Ukrainian Ambassador had also provided one of his diplomats, Igor Kuzhma, a friend of Dr. Yatskiv's, to show us around.

About 30 kilometres northeast of Baku there was a Zoroastrian temple believed to have been built by Persians, but destroyed by Muslims in the 7th century. In the 18th century, Parsees from India came to do business and had the temple rebuilt. The present structure dates from about 1825 and there is a sign in Devanagari script that discloses the temple's Indian origins. Under the main dome of worship, there was an impressive living "sacred flame" that I was told never stops burning. It was probably fuelled by a gas outlet, as there are no Parsees left in Baku to maintain the flame. It seemed appropriate that such a place was still a thriving heritage site in such a surprisingly cosmopolitan country as Azerbaijan.

19

HOME

••

I first began having difficulty pronouncing certain words, especially those that had three consonants in a row such as "S-T-R" (as in "strategy") when I was posted in Poland. I remember it was 1998, during Christmas dinner with the children who were visiting us for the occasion that I noticed I was faltering over some words. I did not think much of it then, but in the summer of 1999 after I'd returned to Ottawa for consultation, I was curious enough to ask Dr. Keith Chang what it meant and whether it was symptomatic of something more serious. He said it sounded like it may be a transient ischemic attack (TIA), a kind of "mini-stroke" that doesn't leave any lasting damage.

Back in Warsaw, I had an appointment with Dr. Friedman, a neurologist, to check it out. He said he'd detected less blood flow to the brain in my left artery and suggested taking aspirin. Dr. Friedman also suggested an X-Ray and a MRI, but these tests didn't show anything was wrong. So, having ruled out tumour, stroke, and concussion, he was at a loss. By 2002, when we moved to Kiev, the problem persisted and in a casual conversation with Dr. Bohdan Karvchenko, the rector of Ukrainian Academy of Public Administration (UAPA), I mentioned that I bit my cheeks and tongue more frequently. He set up an appointment with Dr. Liudmila Verbova who checked several of my reflexes, and said that I might have ALS. I had no idea what ALS meant. After EMG testing of my muscles, she said she was almost sure that I had it. Later that year, when I was in Taiwan, I asked my cousin Yoyo, or Dr. Chiwan Lai, to check me out and he confirmed Dr. Verbova's diagnosis after administering an MRI, EMG, and a muscular biopsy. I was surprised and distressed, but since my bodily functions were intact, I did not take it too seriously. It was Hengching and the children who were very upset, losing sleep and crying at night. I decided I was not going to let the disease get me down, and that I should maintain a high spirit. While I would share the fact of my illness with friends and family, I was determined not to dwell on it. Anyways, who wants to hear a sick man whine about his condition? I had better things to talk about with my friends.

By the end of 2003, my pronunciation was getting increasingly worse and I also started to notice some weakening in the muscles of my neck and arms. I was still able to take brisk, long walks, but I decided to terminate my posting in Ukraine and return to Canada where I could be with my children and where the medical treatment I required was more easily accessible. Although I would have liked to stay on and my bosses were anxious to keep me in Kiev, I decided that the CIDA program in Ukraine deserved a director who was not encumbered by such a serious illness. My staff at the Canadian Embassy was saddened by the prospect of my departure, but I reminded them that nobody is indispensable and that I did not want to leave, but felt I had to go. We left Kiev almost in tears, and arrived in Ottawa in October 2004.

Since my return to Canada, I moved to Toronto in the summer of 2005 and have been visiting the ALS Centre at the Sunnybrook Hospital. My friend Eiji was worried, and he mobilized his network to search for a possible cure. One of his daughters, Deana, found a Chinese hospital that administered stem-cell therapy, and Eiji told me about their program. I asked another friend in Beijing, Adam Williams, to look into it and he recommended Dr. An Yihua of the Armed Police Hospital. To date, I have visited Dr. An's clinic four times: in September of 2005, May of 2006, October of 2006, and December of 2007. When I discussed my visits with Dr. Zinman of Sunnybrook, he opposed my receiving the stem-cell therapy on the grounds that the method was untested. But there were no alternatives and rather than wait for certain death, I decided to take the risk. When I provided Dr. Zinman with a full report of my treatment at the Armed Police Hospital in China, he said that as a doctor he opposed it, but if he were a patient he might do exactly the same thing.

Meanwhile, the disease continued to progress and by November 2008, I was no longer able to walk, and I had to rely on a feeding tube and a breathing machine while in bed. As I continue to weaken, my energy level has declined to the point that it is now difficult to even type these words. Still, throughout this debilitating illness, I maintain my high spirits. When friends or family visit, I talk about them rather than about myself and my condition. We also discuss the topics I have always been passionate about, world affairs, history, and culture. This helps keep my visitors amused, and I think it encourages them to visit me again.

* * *

Life does not wait for illnesses and the sufferings of retired diplomats. No, life goes on and children grow-up and grandchildren are born to new experiences, emotions, and achievements. I used to say that before Nadia was born, we did not want a child. But Nadia gave us so much joy and we fell so completely in love with her, that she made us want more children.

I was not smitten by James Creaner when he first entered the world in September, 2000. Nor was I especially thrilled by Sarah when she arrived in December, 2002. But as Nadia's baby boy and girl grew into bigger and beautiful children, they have become a great source of joy for me. I feel their presence has filled a larger than proportionate part of my life. I thought I'd derived tremendous happiness from my own children, but I was surprised by the degree of pleasure I have found in watching my grandchildren grow.

For some time, I was not at close-range to observe their metamorphosis, and I only heard about their progress from their mother. We lived in Poland until James was two, and then in Ukraine until James was four and Sarah was two. In between, I saw them only twice (Hengching saw them more frequently). When everyone came to Warsaw and I saw James at one-and-a-half, I knew I was head-over-heels in love with him. He was not yet able to talk, but his eyes were already curious and his face was clearly intelligent. I took Nadia, Nina, and Thomas, along with Paul Creaner and Sue Baek to Istanbul for a week, and when we returned, I noticed that James had already grown a bit. I felt a pang of sadness in the knowledge that we would not be witnessing the development of James's intellect more closely. Nadia was (and continues to be) very diligent in keeping me up-to-date. Then, when Sarah came along we realized that we should probably not linger too long overseas. The combination of grandchildren and my advancing ALS led us to decide that I would retire in 2004 so we could be closer to our grandchildren.

James started talking when he was two and a half. In time, his interests grew from dinosaurs to human skeletons, ancient Egyptian, Greek, and Roman mythology. His knowledge of these topics was so extensive that even museum attendants were impressed by his observations and comments. It was most intriguing to observe the development of his mind, but even more impressive was his compassion.

One day, when I let him ride with me on my power wheelchair, he said, "It may feel like a lot of fun, but it is sad if one has to depend on this chair."

For his eighth birthday, James said he did not want any birthday gifts; instead, he wanted his friends to donate to the ALS research fund I established at Sunnybrook Hospital.

Sarah is my "Princesse lointaine," my far away princess. I was able to hold and caress James, but by the time Sarah was old enough for conscious interaction, my arms were no longer strong enough to hold her or even caress her. I look upon her at close range, and yet I felt so remote. When she gives me a hug and a kiss, I cannot not touch her cheeks and hold her close.

Having been born two years after her brilliant brother, Sarah is sometimes unjustly compared to James. It is clear to me that she is quite capable of measuring up to him, both in intellectual acuity and emotional maturity. She has benefited from James's interest in books, and his incessant barrage of stories, facts, and figures. One would think Sarah might turn away and not listen to such a tirade of information. But she is listening and absorbing the most important parts, and she will sometimes even fill in the gaps in James's story-telling (and retelling) when her older brother forgets what comes next.

One of the most wonderful things about Sarah is her optimism. I believe she is the type of person who will always see the cup as half full. Once, James and Sarah opened their fortune cookies after a meal, and neither one found a paper fortune inside. James immediately expressed disappointment, but Sarah said, "It doesn't matter, it tastes the same."

Her attitude towards the uncertainty of one's fortunes is a fitting way to end my story. Even though I am bed-ridden and cannot walk or feel the soft skin of my beautiful grandchildren, my mind is alive with sensations and memories, present and the past, perhaps even more alive and rich than ever before. When I think back upon my work and the many pleasures, passions, people, and places I've had the grace and opportunity to experience, my memories are so full and palpable, that even with this frail body I can say, "It doesn't matter, it tastes the same."

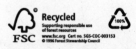

Recycled
Supporting responsible use
of forest resources
FSC   www.fsc.org   Cert no. SGS-COC-003153
© 1996 Forest Stewardship Council

MARQUIS
Marquis Book Printing Inc.

Québec, Canada
2010

Printed on Silva Enviro 100% post-consumer EcoLogo certified paper,
processed chlorine free and manufactured using biogas energy.